"I found Dorothy and George to be gentle, accepting, theologically trained Christians with a sincere heart to research and critique the most effective understanding of Christian healing. Their simple approach is informed both by neuroscience and the idea of practicing the presence of Jesus. It does not engage with the pain story or pain identity from that story until there is a connection with stories of joy, involving an experience of the incarnational God through creation, others, ourselves. This is a rare experience for most of us, particularly for those whose identity has been formed out of stories of neglect or abuse in relationships. A different sense of self unusually blossoms in the telling, recording and listening back. This is gold in my opinion, a tangible experience of being loved by the God of love."

–Vanessa Daughtry,
Clinical Counselor & Lecturer in Counseling

"In this book, healing is about leading people into a revelation of Jesus. In story after story and in the practices set out by Dorothy and George, we see how wonderful our Jesus is. Our Lord is always with us and at work in our lives, even when we've been too distracted by the pressures and pains of this world to be aware of His presence, or have yet to know Him by name. This book is a manual for healers, evangelists and all who desire to minister Jesus. It is a beautiful guide to mining the 'sapphire' truths of His enduring faithfulness, love and greatness in our lives."

–Jennifer, Companion in Prayer

"Dorothy and George Mathieson are an incredible resource for our larger urban poor ministry. They use the bulk of the prayer time to bring people into the presence of Jesus. They hold back from giving advice or problem solving and expect Jesus to lead the time. When we know that Jesus is speaking to us and leading us, hope becomes real, joy is built, and old scars become signs of His healing. This process feels slower, messier, unpredictable, but it actually helps break the pattern of people seeing their identity revolve around their pain."

–Pastor Chris Rattay, New Life Community Church, Los Angeles

"Dorothy and George offer a unique and life-changing approach to the ministry of healing. They define healing as no more or less than experiencing the presence of Jesus. Their decades of sacrificial ministry and mission and vulnerability in personal healing have shaped CompanionLIFE. Their work gently integrates the ministry of healing with empowerment—all followers of Jesus, regardless of their level of formal training, can live out of their friendship with Jesus by being companions to others in their healing journeys. Over the years I have had several profound personal experiences of Jesus' presence while praying with George and Dorothy. But the greatest blessing by far has been learning how to connect with Jesus more in the midst of my regular daily life. May you experience Jesus' presence as you read this book and become a healing companion to others in Jesus' name."

–Lisa Engdahl, Co-General Director of Servant Partners

SEEDS
OF
JOY

SEEDS
OF
JOY

THE HEALING POWER
OF STORY-PRAYER

DOROTHY MATHIESON, PhD

SERVANT PARTNERS PRESS

Servant Partners is an interdenominational evangelical missions agency that
sends, trains, and equips those who follow Jesus by living among the world's
urban poor. By the power of the Holy Spirit, we seek the transformation of
communities with the urban poor through church planting, community
organizing, and leadership development.

Cover and Book design: Loren A. Roberts/HearkenCreative (*hearkencreative.
com*)

Scripture quotations from THE MESSAGE. Copyright © by Eugene H. Peterson
1993, 1994, 1995, 1996, 2000, 2001, 2002. Used by permission of NavPress. All
rights reserved. Represented by Tyndale House Publishers, Inc.

print ISBN: 978-0-9983665-0-0 (ISBN 13)

CONTENTS

INTRODUCTION

THE MAIN CHALLENGE of prayer healing is this: How do we connect people to divine healing resources when they're convinced that God has abandoned them in their pain?

In over 40 years of missional and pastoral ministry, I have never seen Jesus fail to appear in the stories of hurting people. My conviction is that God has placed healing seeds in every person's story, and we are privileged to companion people as they rediscover these seeds. My husband George and I discovered these personally crafted, divinely created healing seeds in our own stories first. Then, over a lifetime of listening to the stories of others, we gradually developed a process that empowered us and many others to become story-healing companions.

It's been a great joy to see so many people grow confident that they, too, can help others discover the power of narrative prayer. We now offer this CompanionLIFE prayer process, as we have called it, for you to freely use and adapt in your own context as well.

My Story of Healing

MY CHILDHOOD HOME was filled with recently released criminals, recovering alcoholics, resting missionaries, and unofficial foster children. My parents provided a loving community long before "community" became a buzz word in church circles. They worked tirelessly for the restoration of many broken people, but always introduced our guests simply as friends. I grew up assuming everyone lived this way.

One Christmas, an ex-criminal carpenter guest delighted me with a fabulous doll's house. It represented months of secret work and was modeled on my favorite house in an upmarket Brisbane suburb. As we drove past, I'd always say, "That's my house," and then, by a seeming miracle, it was. My doll's house story continues to assure me that every person is a potential contributor to our healing. The ex-criminal, my friend, never knew that for over 50 years many other little girls enjoyed his doll's house and experienced in it the joy that is essential to healing.

Healing was mentioned in my father's preaching only in the context of those spurring-on-the-gospel stories of the early disciples. But this theology did not preclude Jesus' healing presence at our communal Sunday lunches. Among others, Mrs. McGuckin usually attended while my father searched for her alcoholic husband on the streets. Eventually they were reunited, found faith, and spent their remaining years together. No elaborate declaration of healing—just doing what Jesus would do.

Many guests to our home were restored in this quiet manner. However, as some guests returned to their old ways and others committed suicide, father pondered in his old age if it had all been worthwhile. When the stories were unfinished, senseless, I'd hear him sigh deeply, "Come, precious Lord Jesus, come." Jesus was my parents' source of patient endurance for the mystery of the usually long healing journey—only the presence of "precious Lord Jesus." He is still that source for me.

After happy times with missionaries in our home, my call to mission seemed to be absorbed naturally with my breakfast cereal. In my early missionary days teaching at a Bible college in Papua New Guinea, I was amazed at the revival stories of the trainee pastors from their practical ministries: stories of healings, fording swollen rivers, speaking languages they'd never learned, releasing demons. Our task was to continue to teach that these demons were fear-based imaginations indicating a lack of biblical knowledge, which of course we could excellently remedy. Then on a retreat, one of my well-taught students had a demonic attack. This time I was the untaught one. "Do something, Jesus!" was my frightened cry. He did more than something. She was released, and my script of New Testament healing began to be decisively re-written.

Still, I was not aware of my own need for healing. Persistent heartaches about singleness, people-pleasing, striving to serve, and dumbing down to win approval were all subdued under busy sacrificial service. I was in my thirties and lecturing at an Asian leaders' conference when a fellow missionary finally said, "You need the baptism of the Holy Spirit for all these internal tensions." I was quite shocked at her noticing my confusions and was unsure of her theology, but she was lovely and gently prayed for me. My surprising response was a new language, new joy, and a new song which I quickly wrote down and later sang to the conference (a minor miracle for a non-musician).

Not long after, my first husband died after one year of marriage. Most Christians had nothing to say to me other than that it shouldn't have happened to someone who'd lived so sacrificially. Then two older ladies offered me weekly healing prayer so I wouldn't be crippled for life by this devastating shock. My theological credentials hardly embraced their labelling every aspect of my pain a demonic spirit that needed to be cast out. However, their loving companionship silenced any theological critique as all sorts of accumulated fears and lonely striving for male acceptance tumbled out.

After a year of prayer healing, my friends declared me healed enough to go on, and they felt I was called to a healing ministry. Was this true? Later that day in my lonely house, I sensed Jesus the Healer come close and assure me that I hadn't been abandoned by this death, but released to offer similar loving, healing companionship to many people.

Right then His healing presence poured into a memory of when I was 18 and a leader at a Christian camp where a doctor talked on sex. Later in personal conversation, the doctor told a friend and me that we were too intelligent, too un-alluring to ever attract a man. Imprinted from then on in my longing young heart was this notion: love will be hard to get. My husband's death triggered this old fear-based conclusion. Would I ever be loved again? There was no specific answer or assurance of another marriage, but the healing presence of Jesus softened that old fear of anticipated loneliness. In Bible teaching and pastoral ministries I could confidently assure hurting, lonely women: Jesus embraced me in my pain—let's ask Him to assure you too of His presence.

Years later, as a missionary in a Manila slum with Servants to Asia's Urban Poor, my status as a widow (not my doctorate, not my theology degree, not my roles as pastor or lecturer) became my most endearing qualification to my poor neighbors. They considered me like themselves: deserted and longing for love. Our shared abandonment fused our healing journeys. No scurrying for solutions, but singing together, "How sweet is the name of Jesus..." as we swatted mosquitos in the power outages and shared the simplest delicious meals. Gradually I was being wooed way beyond a limited theology of healing, in which I would use my gifts to help others, to healing as a together-encounter with the Healer Himself, precious Jesus.

It was also in Manila's slums that seeds for physical healing were planted by my bold, faith-filled slum neighbors. One Sunday in our little slum church, a blind lady walked in asking for healing—quite a usual church event there. "Jesus is here to heal you," the people assured her with their ecstatic singing and uncontrollable shaking, which they said was a sign of the Spirit. Embarrassed, I distanced myself, but they drew me into the healing circle, assuming I was used to praying for the blind to see. I mumbled some apologetic prayer filled with cautious caveats. With their shaking and wild praying, I wasn't really sure who needed healing more desperately: the blind lady or the out-of-control worshippers. Then they asked the lady what color blouse I was wearing. Red, she said, and she was right.

I continued to join their nightly healing forays in the slums, still hesitant about their theology but amazed at the miracles. Huge thyroids disappeared. Twisted limbs were restored. And my narrow-mindedness was healed. No longer would I try to manage healing or rigidly categorize its types (physical/emotional/spiritual). Jesus is far too creative, too theology-shattering for that. It's all about asking, "What do You want to do today, Lord Jesus?"

After my happy one year of marriage cut short by death, I entered confidently thirteen years later into my second marriage with George. I was Dorothy, and Dorothy means, "God's Gift." I had prayed for the blind to see. I had spoken at huge charismatic rallies and prayed for many to be released from their burdens. In my estimation, marriage difficulties were in the minor league of miracles. Any problem that surfaced, I'd confidently say to George, "You can be healed in the name of Jesus right now."

My sensitive husband was not impressed! "Living with you is like being in a constant charismatic convention. Even your prayers are manipulating me to change," he said. Deeply disturbed, I apologized. It was clear that my earlier discovery of the mutuality of healing had not taken deep root. It was also achingly clear that my confidence in quick solutions was more about my fear of not coping, rather than about my trusting Jesus to accompany us on His unique healing journey in our marriage. Into my own story gradually dawned a different basis for healing, way beyond theological correctness and control, to intimate, vulnerable, healing relationships—with my husband, others, and Jesus.

Our healing has opened up the wide horizons of grace-filled loving and doing prayer ministry together. In ministries to international students, and then training Teachers of English to Speakers of Other Languages (TESOL) for mission, this became our sustaining motto: join in the work Jesus is already doing in people's lives. He is at work; it's His work. We are His companions—with eyes wide open for what He will do next.

Seeking a Model for Prayer Healing

THIS IS THE SPIRIT in which we attended a mission conference about 15 years ago. George and I thought we were there to call others to mission as usual, but we were surprised when we received a call to companion people who were longing for healing from their often-secret burdens: pastors crippled by sexual addictions, missionaries striving hard to compensate for past failings, mothers blaming themselves for the mental illness in their adult children, theology students finding no healing in their academics. Over and over, we heard their cry: could they ever be released from the conflict of unruly, inner turmoil to serve God in freedom?

From that point on, George and I studied, attended seminars, examined and experienced many healing models, and prayed with whomever the Lord sent to us. John 14:10 became our conviction: that we want to cooperate with Jesus in the healing work He is doing and wants to do. The healing ministry of Jesus is for all Christians. Just do it, says James 5:14. Christians asking for prayer healing is—or at least ought to be—as normal as singing.

7

In our journey, we had two dreams. Firstly, we wanted to develop a user-friendly prayer healing model for evangelical Christians. Many pastors are afraid to venture into the conflicting waters of theological debate and potential church splits over healing. Yet they agree that their churches are full of unhealed people. To make the model accessible, we wanted to avoid the use of extra-biblical concepts and emphasize the church as the foundational healing community. The aim of healing as nothing less than revival is George's constant prayer.

Our other dream was to promote prayer healing in mission. Inspiring this call were the healing stories of workers with so-called "unreached peoples" in other cultures, including the stories in my own history. After trying to teach correct doctrine without much fruit, these missionaries have taken a different approach: they ask people, "Would you like to meet Jesus personally in your pain?" Healing prayer in the name of Jesus bypassed cognitive and cultural defenses to enable many to be touched. Some become overt, others secret disciples. We wished we'd discovered prayer healing as a basis for cross-cultural ministry much earlier.

To carry out these dreams, we needed a process that would be accessible to all. From the multiple gifts of healing described in scripture (1 Corinthians 12:9, 12:28, 12:30), we gradually learned God was leading us toward prayer healing for emotional pain, though this often leads to physical healing.

As we sought information about emotional healing, we came across godly neuroscientists and neurotheologians who have challenged us: if God made the brain to process pain in a certain way, why don't we do prayer healing that way? Often in early prayer healing, we had rushed with people into their stories of trauma—because pain is so consuming, demanding attention. This new challenge encouraged us instead to invite people first into the presence of Jesus, then into their stories of joy, and only later into their stories of trauma. This breakthrough provided the distinctive piece that has opened the door for so many to find safe story pathways to healing in Jesus.

When one severely abused person realized that not all sections of the church advocated a healing ministry, she looked stunned. "Tell them to get a life," she said. We took this advice personally. That simple word, LIFE, resonated with us. It clarified our call to companion as many as possible to life-transforming healing.

And thus, the CompanionLIFE process emerged. Though boundlessly flexible, our prayer sessions consistently follow four major steps:

L Live in the Presence of Jesus

I Identify Past Stories of His Presence

F Find Him in Those Moments Where He Seemed Absent

E Express Thanks to Him

We are thankful for this rhythm because it is replicable, teachable, and adaptable. We invite you to read and absorb what we've learned of each stage, integrating as much as you'd like into your own life and ministry.

Use of This Book

THIS BOOK AIMS to equip the reader with the tools to find healing seeds in your own stories, to walk with others in this work, and to host supportive groups of prayer healing. People of all theological and educational backgrounds have found this process powerful and accessible. Essential to the LIFE process is a willingness to meet Jesus as Healer in our own lives first.

As the name suggests, the idea of companionship is central in the CompanionLIFE process, and I do recommend reading this book with others who will walk toward healing with you. If that is not available, I would encourage you to find trusted friends or mentors who can listen to and support what you are learning about yourself, about story healing, and about Jesus as you read. Though companionship can be inconvenient, vulnerable, and even counter-cultural, it really is a central piece in our healing.

An important note here is that this model does not imitate or replace professional therapy. Trauma psychotherapy, with its diagnoses, treatment plans, and sense of the practitioner's authority, is the domain of licensed professionals. But a peer companion in mutual healing can play a key role in empowering others to face even the most horrific trauma, and even the bewildering saga of mental illness. We are humbled by referrals from therapists who recognize that their clients need to build joy and quiet in the presence of Jesus before they can move forward. A storytelling friendship with Jesus and others has blessed countless people on their journey to mental health.

We rarely engage this process with children under the age of 16. The basic principles behind the LIFE rhythm are more firmly in place in adult brains. In our experience, the greatest healing resource we can offer to children is equipping parents with healing habits that they can model and teach to their children. We trust that children in healed homes may grow into adults who are equipped to process pain by living in the presence of Jesus.

On a final note, we deeply recommend that narrative healing prayer be offered freely and without charge. It's our conviction that we shouldn't charge people for the work that Jesus is doing in them. Our payment is the joy of companioning many into the presence of Jesus.

What's Inside

THE FOUR SECTIONS of this book follow the four phases of the CompanionLIFE rhythm. Each section has three chapters that explore the theory and practice of that phase. You'll find illustrative stories from real CompanionLIFE sessions. Exercises also confirm that the healing process is both a present (God's part) and a practice (our part).

Due to the sensitive nature of many prayer sessions, names are almost always changed and other identifying information has been removed from stories. But every story quoted here is both true and deeply precious to us.

The appendix contains activities, further reading, and other resources for prayer healing. A fuller library of the tools we use can be found at this book's website, *www.ServantPartnersPress.org/SeedsOfJoy.*

We hope this book will provide new insights into the power of narrative prayer, deepening the joyful celebration of the healing seeds in our stories. I did my best to cite any ideas that were traceable back to original sources; however, the insights absorbed over the years have become so integrated into the model and into who I am that citations are likely not complete. I respectfully ask the grace of those whose insights comprise the lineage of this model.

This journey of story-healing continues to be transformational within our own lives and ministry. We pray it will be so for you also.

PART ONE:

LIVE IN THE PRESENCE OF JESUS

1

HEALING IS CONNECTING TO JESUS

LIVING IN THE PRESENCE of Jesus is our only qualification for ministry.

Nothing else—no credential, no external affirmation, and certainly no book—can empower us to walk with others toward life restoration. Transformative healing is connecting the Jesus who "heals the broken-hearted and bandages their wounds" (Psalm 147:3), who shows the greatest love anyone has ever known by laying down His life for His friends (John 15:3). We are healed "by His stripes" (Isaiah 53:5), and the root of the word for "stripes" is related to the word "friend" in modern Hebrew.[1] By His friendship we are healed. And only by His friendship can we offer His friendship, His healing, to others.

A woman who recently came for prayer told my husband and me, "I can see that a Jesus focus, not a pain focus, guides every aspect of your ministry. I never thought that my story would connect me to Jesus like this." Our hope is that if our CompanionLIFE prayer process is distinguished by anything, it is this: every participant in our ministry and yours reconnects with Jesus, their Healer and Friend, in their stories.

Connecting or reconnecting comes first and builds our joy foundations for healing. If you are aching for immediate solutions, or if you work with people who want healing without connections, this beginning might bring up feelings of impatience. But neuroscience has taught us that joy is essential for healthy brains, and that by first securing ourselves in joy-filled companionship (with peers-in-healing and with Jesus Himself), we can successfully move through places of great pain and onward into more healing. Our process celebrates both Jesus' promised friendship and His incredible design of our brains, enabling us to build joy and quiet with Jesus, others, and ourselves.

In this sense, 'Live in the Presence of Jesus' is both the first step of any prayer process, and the constant aim of the entire project. See if you can't find Jesus' presence in all four phases of the CompanionLIFE rhythm:

The CompanionLIFE Process[2]

A PRAYER SESSION is almost always initiated by the person seeking healing. We recommend two prayer leaders, male and female, as a safe combination for hurting people. We also encourage the person to invite a supportive, non-relative companion if possible.

L - Live in the Presence of Jesus

The prayer leader explains the aim of prayer healing: to live in the presence of Jesus. The person seeking healing tells the reason for asking for prayer ministry, and outlines some details of their pain. If present, the companion will be prompted to introduce themselves and their friendship to the person seeking healing. The leader affirms Jesus' presence is the only source of healing the person's true identity. The leader or companion welcomes His presence by anointing with oil, sometimes communion. Those present then build joy before quieting in prayer together.

I - Identify Past Stories of His Presence

The person seeking healing is prompted to tell in detail a specific story when they sensed the presence of Jesus. The leader then asks the person to reflect on their story by asking, "What were you like in the presence of Jesus?" and "How did He treat you?"

This story contains the seeds of healing needed for current pain. It is so vital, in fact, that the prayer companion will tell the story back to the person prayerfully, slowly, so they can re-encounter the presence of Jesus and absorb more deeply what they discovered about themselves and Jesus in His presence.

F - Find Him in Those Moments When He Seemed Absent

The person is invited or prompted to tell stories related to the wounds that brought them to the session, often stories where Jesus' presence is unclear or unrealized. The companion/leader will ask Jesus to restore His presence in the person's area of pain, to come as He did in the person's first story. Those present wait together to see what Jesus will do.

E - Express Thanks to Him

The person seeking healing and their companion/leader celebrate the way Jesus has restored His presence in the person's pain. Connections to a relevant biblical story will enhance the value of the person's story and build courage to pursue lifelong healing. Certificates and other mementos can help to mark the person's journey.

This outline is not a rigid checklist, but a rhythm that has become comfortable and meaningful to us over time. Often we don't complete the whole rhythm in a single session. We might spend several weeks building joy, building capacity to connect to the presence of Jesus, before someone is even ready to face their pain. We might hold sessions in a home, office, or out in nature. They might involve painting, singing, movement, or anything else that feels appropriate and comfortable.

The following brief accounts of real prayer sessions will enrich your appreciation of the variations of the process.

Session 1: A Lion Story

SEVERAL YEARS AGO, my husband George and I were delighted to meet Josie, a missionary with an incredible ministry among child soldiers. She was renowned, credentialed, and yet personally *aching* for safety. We respected her ministry at home and overseas, but didn't know anything about her needs.

L - Live in the Presence of Jesus

We began by articulating our assurance that Jesus would guide the process. We asked Josie what she liked about Jesus. "He defends me," she said. We recognized the connection to her presenting need for safety. We quieted together with Josie by repeating the phrase, "Thank You, Jesus. You are my Defender," while she breathed slowly, deeply. We prayed this simple prayer a number of times slowly, the first half of the prayer said as she breathed in, the second half as she breathed out, until her body and mind became peaceful. As this integrative preparation for deeper sharing wound down, she unexpectedly began showing us photos of lions that she'd saved on her phone—her favorite animal, she said. Rather than treating this as an interruption, we were thankful for the opportunity to share some of Josie's joy. We didn't need to initiate joy building this time, as she'd done it spontaneously!

I - Identify Past Stories of His Presence

We asked Josie if these lion photos reminded her of Jesus in any way. She shared that her favorite picture of Jesus is as a lion, "like Aslan lying down with me, bearing his teeth, saying, 'Don't come near my kid. I am her Defender.'"[3] We asked Josie what she felt like in the presence of her Defender Jesus. She responded, "With Him I feel protected and secure, even in all my mission ventures and ups and downs." We then paused to pray and affirm Josie's description of Jesus, that she was protected in the presence of

Jesus, by praying, "Thank You, Jesus, that You are like the great, strong, beautiful lion Aslan, and You defend Josie. Thank You that You lie down with Josie and keep her safe." Then we asked if she had any more lion stories, and we enjoyed these together.

F - Find Him in Those Moments When He Seemed Absent

Then Josie remembered a pain story—a story from almost 40 years ago, when she was just 11 years old and had never heard of Jesus. She had seen the movie *Born Free* and fell in love with Elsa, the beautiful lioness. "My heart leapt. I wanted to live on the edge like her. Lions to me were safe, but people weren't. I can hardly believe it now, but Elsa inspired me to say no to my Grandfather's secret abuse."

We might have asked Josie to reflect on Jesus' involvement in this story, but she did this spontaneously: "No wonder I later came to love Jesus, the Lion," she said. "He's been my safe Defender and still is as I go into risky mission to defend others." Then we stopped to pray thanks to God for giving courage to Josie to say no to her grandfather's abuse through the story of the lioness Elsa, and to Jesus for revealing Himself as Josie's faithful and defending Lion, and the Holy Spirit for revealing these healing insights.

E - Express Thanks to Him

Josie was overjoyed to realize that Jesus was active in her story before she ever met Him—and that He was still her Defender. We celebrated this by Josie's retelling more recent stories where she had seen this wonderful quality of Jesus. She realized that she could stay centered through focusing daily on Jesus her Defender in quieting prayer. Josie has since told us that she recognizes signs of God's healing Lion-friendship in ordinary daily events: challenging meetings, disappointed mission outcomes, family dilemmas. We wrote out Josie's story on a certificate, honoring and celebrating Jesus' friendship in her life, and Josie now lives out of a deepened gratitude to her Defender.

Session 2: Hope in Healing Water

ELANA CAME TO US for prayer healing with a trusted companion. Though she was part of Australia's middle class, she said she needed a safe path out of a war-zone life—the bitter private and internal wars of her personal devastation. She felt had never connected with God in relationship, but I would learn that she had a powerful story about Him.

L - Live in the Presence of Jesus

Like many people, Elana came to the session expecting to focus on her pain. As soon as she sat down, awful stories began to tumble out—stories of an outwardly Christian but incredibly cruel father, stories of a controlling husband too much like her father, stories of a severely disabled daughter whom she felt helpless to care for. As soon as we could do so without cutting her off, we asked if we might pause to quiet. We would do this by having the companion Elana had brought along with her affirm Elana in prayer. She thanked Jesus for Elana's courage and strength—Elana was a teacher, her companion shared in prayer, who stayed present with her students in the worst of her pain. Hearing this affirmation began to build Elana's joy.

I - Identify Past Stories of His Presence

It was then easier to ask Elana to tell us a story where she sensed the presence of Jesus. We quieted again through deep breathing, and focusing on the characteristic of Jesus she connected to: His strength. After this, what she remembered was remarkable. "A friend gave me some holy water from Lourdes to help my daughter. *'What hocus-pocus,'* I thought, and left it on the shelf. One day while she was fitting terribly, I cried out, 'God if You can forgive me, if You think we're worthwhile, allow me some connection.' I grabbed the Lourdes water and poured it over myself. I was at the end of the line. At that very moment I met a Father of love (not like my father), a haven, not judging me, just waiting for me." We responded with celebration and affirmation of her sense of God being a good Father to her. Her companion repeated her story back to her in a prayer of thanksgiving, giving Elana a chance to focus on this healing connection.

F - Find Him in Those Moments When He Seemed Absent

We then asked Elana if there were any similarities between her life during the time of the story and now. She responded that not much has outwardly changed since then—perhaps her pain was at a 10 out of 10 in that moment, and now it was an 8 out of 10. Still intense, and still incredibly wearying. We asked the Father of Love to come into her heartbroken current story. We quieted our bodies and minds in silence long enough for this to happen.

E - Express Thanks to Him

Elana said, "I can see that my connection to God the Father of Love, to Jesus, is real, and that I need to keep it up every day." Though it took years for new medical insights to help stabilize her daughter, her deepened connection both to God and to her companion sustained her in more joy and peace along the way.

Session 3: I Got the Answer

IN OUR TRAVELS to the United States, George and I frequently visit a cross-class urban church in Los Angeles that has adopted us as its grandparents. At one point, Gustavo, a new Christian and a member of the church, was grappling with massive anger problems. He attended a CompanionLIFE seminar and afterwards asked for a session with us.

L - Live in the Presence of Jesus

Gustavo brought his mentor, Pastor Chris, to the session as his companion. We started by asking Chris and Gus what they enjoyed about each other. They had a lot of joy to share! Gus quieted by breathing deeply in and out, and as he did, praying to Jesus, "Thank you, Jesus, I am loved." We then laid hands on him and prayed this same prayer along with him.

I - Identify Past Stories of His Presence

When we asked Gustavo to share a story of Jesus showing up in his life, he took about 40 minutes to tell us five back-to-back stories. He just couldn't stop talking about how much Jesus had changed his life. His companion Chris looked concerned that we were never going to get to any pain because of his nonstop joyful sharing!

F - Find Him in Those Moments When He Seemed Absent

When he wound down, we asked Gus about his reason for visiting. He quickly brought up a key moment in his 'anger story.' Some years ago, his wife gave birth early to their only daughter, but she lived for just six hours. He held her before she died, but this just increased the pain of losing her—he was angry at God and at the hospital, which wouldn't intervene because of his lack of insurance.

We asked Gus if he would be willing to go back to that moment when he was holding his daughter and ask Jesus to come. When both Gus and Chris tensed up, we asked them to recall the goodness of Jesus in his many joy stories. Then Gus looked to the ground and fidgeted for about a minute of very awkward silence. Finally, he looked up and said, "Ok, I'll try."

My husband asked Chris to lead the quieting prayer. Chris stood next to Gus's chair and placed one hand on Gus's forehead, the other on the back of his neck—a comforting and tension-relieving gesture. Chris slowly repeated the phrase, "Thank You, Jesus, You give me answers."

As Chris finished, Gustavo started giggling! He blurted out, "I got the answer. I got the answer I've been looking for all these years! Jesus just told me that He didn't rob me of my daughter! He *gave* her to me—for six whole hours! My wife and I got six hours to meet and hold and love our baby girl before she went to Jesus. He loves me!"

E - Express Thanks to Him

We were all in awe at this revelation. Through six months of mentoring Gus, Chris had never even considered saying anything like this to Gus—and of course he couldn't have. Only Jesus could tell Gus what His heart was. Our small part was guiding Gus in giving Jesus space to do that, and He had been faithful.

We closed the session in praise to the Jesus who gives answers—deeply satisfying, unexpected answers. Now, instead of viewing this moment in his life as one of his most painful, Gus sees it as one of the most precious gifts Jesus has given him. It has become one among his growing collection of joy stories as the roots of his anger continue to disappear. Chris and Gus now lead healing teams to many disadvantaged communities. Healing multiplies through Gus's healing.

These three stories illustrate that the CompanionLIFE process is all about re-connecting with the presence of Jesus. It is the first step, and in this book it is the first chapter, but we will regularly and intentionally return to the presence of Jesus throughout every phase of this process and in every chapter of this book.

Your Healing Is Your Best Gift to Others

IN OUR EXPERIENCE, it is exceedingly easy to forget that we are not the healers in the prayer process. We are recipients of healing, inviting others to be healed along with us. To make this true and meaningful, we must take the vulnerable path of seeking our own healing first.

There are two reasons for my adamant recommendation that any prayer companion receive prayer healing before praying for others. The first is that no matter how well any person seems to function, we all carry pain and disconnection within us. The only meaningful variable from person to person is whether we invite Jesus into our unique burdens.

The second reason is that we can relate to anyone seeking healing so much better when we too live in the presence of Jesus and regularly and humbly admit our healing needs. In prayer we test what comforts us; we feel the ache of waiting for Jesus to appear in our pain stories. This qualifies us to be true empathetic companions in another person's healing.

This is a key reason that I recommend reading this book with others. We practice both the presence of Jesus, and the specific tools in this book, most effectively with a partner or community. We can't be healed alone. Many times, it will make sense to take turns guiding and receiving prayer and instruction with a partner or group. If you are reading alone, seek out friends to try different applications with you along the way.

Activities for Application

1. Reflect on the three session examples earlier in this chapter. Which person seeking healing reminds you most of yourself? Which encounter reminds you most of the way Jesus has appeared in your own life?

2. Reflect on the CompanionLIFE rhythm. Does the LIFE process remind you of anything you've tried or experienced before? Does any phase or aspect of the process seem particularly valuable for meeting your needs and the needs of your community?

3. Practice the CompanionLIFE rhythm within yourself. You may have already picked up some tools and principles to infuse in your prayers with others, and you will certainly pick up more along the way. For now, flip to the adapted personal script in Appendix A and try it in your next prayer time.

---

[1] Stripes: Chabburah (Strong's *Greek Lexicon* #H2250); Friend: xaver (modern Hebrew).

[2] This is a basic introduction to the rhythm of CompanionLIFE. Sample scripts are found in Appendix A.

[3] Aslan refers to the God figure in the *Chronicles of Narnia* series by C. S. Lewis.

2

JOY CONNECTIONS

IN OUR EARLY EXPLORATIONS into prayer healing, George and I focused on peoples' stories of pain. Pain is so urgent, so demanding of relief, and we really had seen ourselves as compassionate pain relievers—with Jesus, of course! But now, we have come to see ourselves as Helpers of Joy, borrowed from Paul in 2 Corinthians 1:24. We choose to be facilitators of a connection with Jesus, our Joy Giver, and our Originator of Joy.

Our inspiration for this change in focus came from Christian neuroscientists and neurotheologians who were also committed to healing with Jesus. They taught us that our brain flourishes on joy. We crave and seek it out; we're wired for it. Joy is where we belong, and where we are fully ourselves—at our best.

Joy is always relational. It says, "I'm glad to be with you."[4] We need to hear that from Jesus, others, and ourselves. Right from conception we should have been immersed in joy. But joy deficits continue to show up in aching gaps in our sense of belonging, responding, connecting, maturing, and finding our true calling.[5] As a result, we can't process our pain—in fact, our brains only heal when our joy is greater than our pain.

It's no surprise that a joy-over-pain approach is giving us, along with professional counselors and therapists, a new way of meeting with people. Below is one counselor's reflection after she accompanied her client to try this joy-focused healing with us:

> The remarkable thing is that George and Dorothy did not engage my client's pain story at all over her two sessions. I heard important stories of ways out of difficult situations, stories of God's affirmation of her meaning and purpose—none of which I had heard in all our time together! A different sense of self blossomed in the telling and re-telling. This is gold in my opinion, a tangible experience of being loved by the God of love.

This counselor's statement reminds us that we Christians are not struggling to build our joy capacity or our joy connections alone. We are reconnecting with the God of love, drawing on the resources of our Joy Giver—Jesus, our Healer. Awareness of His presence in us is the source of overflowing, enveloping, healing joy (2 Peter 1:16-18).

One of my favorite insights about joy with Jesus comes from His greeting the two women after they found His empty tomb (Matthew 28:9). The angel's assurance of His resurrection hadn't fully softened their debilitating fears. Then they met Jesus, who greeted them with, "Joy to you. Rejoice!" (NKJV), a more accurate translation than "Hail" or "Greetings."[6] His call was not the usual "Shalom," not the standard wish for their well-being, not a casual hello. No, this was a surprising greeting, the assured guarantee that He is present in His risen power; the dark night of doubting is over; He is the Lord of their future. "Joy to you," is certain, hope-filled joy, His pledge to us also. A life-transforming greeting from the only One who offers and originates our joy.

It's His joy that builds our joy, that snatches up our controlled distancing, our reluctance at being captured by His continuous presence of joy. As Nehemiah puts it, His joy is our strength (Nehemiah 8:10). An ancient pictograph of that verse presents the joy of God as a door in a fence.[7] True joy derives from God's opening a door even through our barricades, right into His presence. Joy building doesn't originate or depend on our elusive self-determination, but is our privileged grateful response to this invitation to enter into a harmonious relationship with Him. This is our source of strength. His joy door is always open and we are welcomed into the most pleasurable place God has designed for us, His strengthening, joy-filled presence.

We don't want to close the joy door or lose our "relational-joy connections," as Lehman calls them[8]—connections to Jesus, others, and ourselves. Disconnecting kills joy. Connecting builds joy and helps us get out of negative emotions. Joyful connections with safe others open the door to His joy-filled, healing presence.

Establishing Joy in Prayer Sessions

How do we intentionally prepare people for a joy rather than a pain approach to prayer healing? Over the years, we have learned a few ways to establish and keep the session in a tone of meaningful joy. This isn't an inflexible checklist, but a list of techniques that have proved beneficial in our sessions.

Invite Joy Companions

We always ask people to bring a trusted friend (not a family member) to the prayer session if possible. This should be someone who can support them during and after the session, ideally someone with more joy than they have at the moment. At the beginning of our time together, we ask, "What do you enjoy about each other?" This is a natural way both to get acquainted with the person and their companion, and to celebrate the relational joy that is the vital healing resource for any deficits in their sense of belonging.

During the session, the companion is invited to participate at various points: leading quieting prayer (after we model), retelling their friend's stories, and affirming their friend's heart and their self-discoveries in Jesus. At the end, the companion will share what they observed in the session and can also suggest ongoing ways to support their friend.

This companionship celebrates safe, healing, relational joy. For example, Jess invited her companion for prayer about her secret mental turmoil. Even though she was a prayer minister herself, Jess was perplexed: "How do I apply the presence of Jesus to my long history of over-responsibility for everyone, especially my aging mother? Where is God in my long-term chronic fatigue?" We encouraged her to ask Jesus what she asked us. As her friend led her in quieting, this is what came to Jess: "I don't have to hold it all together." Jess then shared beautiful stories of when she was freed from this mental turmoil of holding it all together. Her companion retold these stories and we quieted again to absorb these complex ongoing issues in the presence of Jesus.

At the end of the session, her companion summarized her overview of the session: "I can see we're not searching for a moment of healing, but we're looking for the patterns of hope. In the presence of Jesus, it's a diminishing of negative pathways." We were excited that Jess's companion saw how the presence of Jesus highlighted patterns of hope in her story. Jess was appreciated, heard, and validated in loving companionship—truly a joy foundation for this session and for her ongoing healing journey. Jess and her friend continue to identify and celebrate patterns of hope in the frequent joy conversations that comprise their friendship.

Bring Joy Objects

A favorite object can easily connect people to their own joy, and we love to open up sessions by inviting the person to tell us about what they brought. If we don't remember to ask or if the person doesn't have a chance to bring something, we offer photos to prompt their joy or we might just ask them to recall something tangible. In the age of smartphones, many people are able to pull up their favorite photos and songs instantly, with a similar effect.

Another alternative we've discovered is making simple colored cloths available in our sessions. People can select a color that they associate with joy, even draping it around themselves to embody an immersion in joy. One person associated blue with purity—a joy discovered in Jesus. This led him to pray, "Thank You, Jesus. I'm covered in Your purity, no matter what I've done."

This tangible joy is so essential, grounding the abstract in the real, the experiential. Sometimes we find that people benefit from carrying or re-visiting their joy objects between sessions. For instance, Anna was immensely worried about an upcoming shoulder surgery. Trusting in God was difficult, especially as she had nearly died during the previous surgery. Her joy companions asked her if she had something to take to the hospital to help her to trust.

Immediately, Anna thought of her grandma's cross. Years before, she had carried it from Cornwall as a symbol of trust for beginning her new life in a different country. Passed on through Anna's mother who has since died, the cross is always by her bedside. "I'm at peace now. I know what trust looks like as I go on my own unknown journey. Trust is not a nebulous concept. It's tangible, real." Stories of trust uniting the family (as in Psalm 78:5-7) were embodied in Grandma's cross.

Make Bible Connections

An unexpected connection to a biblical story may provide a joy connection for a lot of people as they express their problems. It may even provide an entry point for someone to begin their healing journey.

One day I set up a prayer booth at a local fair and asked people, "Would you like to meet Jesus today?" Most thought it was a bit of a hoot, but one woman said, "Why not? My partner has left and I'm devastated. I'm like a little boat on a stormy sea. I just wish someone would come and bring me some peace."

Immediately I connected the story of Jesus and the disciples in the storm (Mark 4:39) to this woman's deep longing. I asked her if she would like to hear a Bible story just like hers. "I'd really like that," she sighed. She was amazed how Jesus came into the disciples' fears right in the storm. Then she had her first immersion in the presence of Jesus as we prayed, "Thank You, Jesus, for Your peace."

Tell Life-Affirming Personal Stories

Early in the session, we may ask someone to share stories related to a positive life celebration. For example, we've asked people to tell their birth story, as much as they know—from their own current perspective, from the perspective of their parents, even writing a birth announcement from God's perspective. We've also asked about baptism stories and other spiritually significant moments. All sorts of appreciation stories build up their joy foundations.

Start with Joy Assignments

Since neuroscience has taught us that pain can only heal in the presence of a healthy level of joy, we do not move toward someone's pain if their joy seems to be very low. Instead, we would work with them to establish patterns of joy within and between sessions first.

Some of our consistently assigned joy activities, such as Joy Journaling, Joy People (noticing joy in others), and Joy with Jesus (noticing Jesus daily), are part of our personal collection, commemorated with well-defined certificates. More examples of these are listed in Appendix B.

Other joy building is worked out spontaneously, tailored to the person and the needs of the moment. Elsie was severely disconnected and without joy. She told us, "The only people who have ever liked me are babies." Recognizing that infants were her unique source of joy connection, we arranged for her to work in our church's nursery for six weeks before proceeding with us. This has helped to rebuild her depleted joy resources so that she could enter her past and present pain in a healthier way.

Activities can also build on joy stories shared in sessions. Sally's life was joy-depleted, but we discovered in her stories her courageous missionary grandfather, who bravely endured prison in China for his faith. Her eyes lit up as she told his story. Journaling her joy story was her assignment before our next prayer session.

Begin Joy Groups

Joy is connecting to Jesus, others, and ourselves. We need one another for healing joy. Many have benefited from forming joy-focused groups that quiet, share joy stories, and pray together. Joy groups can precede or supplement individual sessions, and are also an excellent choice for long-term joy maintenance after a series of individual sessions has come to a close. Joy groups, and how to start them, are discussed at greater length in Chapter 11.

Sustain a Lifestyle of Joy

JOY-BUILDING NOT ONLY increases the quality of prayer sessions, but enriches our ordinary routines. Joy is sourced in relating to the resurrected Jesus, so the more we live in His presence, the more joy we have to process our pain, accept the lives we are given, and suffer well.

Becoming a more joyful person can seem like an overwhelming task. The good news is that healing doesn't require absorbing one large, amorphous block of joy. In Psalm 6:11, the Hebrew text puts "joy" in plural form— joy is actually a lot of little joys, which together fill up our capacities. All of our joy tools for prayer sessions are based on this understanding. We can train ourselves to live in joy, return to joy, and build joy through many little joys.

A lifestyle of joy is essential for prayer leaders in their calling to resource others in joy. We need to replenish our joy constantly.

Find Joy in Nature and Your Environment

Many of us find our joy resources refreshed through nature. Whenever I'm in a rainforest where it's silent and the trees arch over me, it's like Jesus is enclosing me tightly in His love. I'm free. When I put my head under the waves and pretend to surf, I feel like Jesus is cleansing me and there's nothing wrong. When I see a rainbow, I remember how God's forgiveness surrounded me in a moment of awful guilt.[9]

Jesus' joy presence can further be prompted in unexpected places: plants fighting through sidewalks, sunlight struggling between buildings, crazily decorated food stands, even graffiti. There is no environment where He isn't present.

Build Joy in Work

It's important for joy to refresh our daily tasks, no matter what our calling. Brian, a well-loved doctor, was feeling helpless as he visited his dying patient. He prayed that this woman, a believer and a nature-lover, would have a final experience of God's care in her agony. Later, her sister related that a bird flew in her window and sang on her bed for half an hour. Joy as she died. Deep joy for Brian who longs for a harmonious unity of his faith and profession.

Years ago as a weary missionary in Manila, I was stuck in a horrible traffic jam. The jeepney I was riding in was belching out the blackest pollution I'd ever seen. I felt intensely the costs of urban ministry. But then I saw two lovers kissing in the front seat of the car. I said to myself, *if they can love here, I too can experience Jesus' love and not be a joyless, frustrated missionary.*

Focus on Joy During Occasions and Events

Birthdays, anniversaries, holidays, and Sunday lunches can be occasions for mutual joy building. For some people, these can be painful, increasingly so with age. Joy prompts can help create a fresh focus at these important events.

Once we were at a friend's 80th birthday morning tea. She was frail and wondering if her life had been worthwhile. To celebrate we said, "Tell us one story from each decade of your life." Over the next two hours, eight amazing stories flowed out—stories of wild youthful motorbike rides with her boyfriend; pioneering music experiences for deaf children; creating beautiful worship music—wonderful, inspiring stories from someone who summed up her life as a depressing mismatch. When we arrived home, the phone rang. "I've got more stories," she said. More joy, more sustenance for aging insecurities. As weakness increased, we had many more joy-filled morning teas with "tell us that story again."

We also celebrate events by singing homemade songs to celebrate birthdays, sports awards, house sales—any occasion. We sing them loudly, with lots of laughs and without worry about rhyming or keeping in tune. We had 27 verses for George's recent birthday song.

Any mile-markers in our lives can be used for this sort of joyful reflection—within ourselves, in conversations, or in groups and parties.

Build Up Joy with Gratitude

Saying thank you builds and refreshes joy. It shifts our focus to appreciate the good in others in an incredibly healing way. Shopping becomes a joy moment when we give a waitress or shop assistant a pearl (from a cheap necklace), saying, "Thank you for your help. This pearl is to remind you how precious you are." None of our pearls have been refused, even with the accompanying scripture card welcomed. Similarly, blessing cards are easily prepared as thank-yous for road workers, construction people, and other helpers. Joy transforms daily inconveniences and easily opens up opportunities for sharing Jesus.

Have Patience in Joy Building

Many of us begin quite low in joy and in joy connections. One pastor said, "I had no idea about building joy. I thought it should just come naturally. When it doesn't, I blame myself." He is not alone. Confessing a lack of joy creates complicated feelings for many Christians. We're embarrassed by our depressions, even feeling as though we've failed to follow the command to be always joy-filled (e.g. Philippians 4:4, Matthew 5:12). But as we gradually deepen our secure connections with Jesus, we surprisingly discover joy even in suffering, even in the hardest times.

"Sharing mutual brokenness" is the way Anna described her source of joy. Her life bridges two mostly irreconcilable worlds—rich White (her birth world) and poor Black (her chosen world of mission). The tension is tough, made harder by the reality that now she feels she belongs to neither. But it's a call to be who she is designed to be: someone who is meaningfully present in a world of suffering. "There is joy in breaking my heart," she concludes.

We must be very quiet to discover this kind of joy, said Bonhoeffer in his prison cell at Christmas time.[10] Next we explore quieting for our healing journey.

Activities for Application

1. Discuss, journal, and/or create something that reflects what you've learned about joy over the years and in this section.

2. Browse the collection of joy exercises in Appendix B. Choose one that appeals to you, and practice it regularly this week.

3. Suggest a few joy exercises to someone who expresses a need for more joy this week. Practice the exercise with them, as appropriate.

---

[4] James Wilder, et al., *Living from the Heart Jesus Gave You* (Pasadena: Shepherd's House, 1999), 22.

[5] These are signs of the brain's pain processing pathway – see Chapter 6.

[6] Strong's *Greek Lexicon* #G5463

[7] Skip Moen, "Open the Gate," *Hebrew Word Study*, June 12, 2010, accessed November 12, 2016, *skipmoen.com/2010/06/open-the-gate/*.

[8] Karl Lehman, "Identifying When You Have Lost Access to Your Relational Connection Circuits, and Getting Them Back On Line," November 12, 2008, accessed November 12, 2016, *www.kclehman.com/download.php?doc=151*.

[9] This story is told in Chapter 9.

[10] Dietrich Bonhoeffer, *I Want to Live These Days with You: A Year of Daily Devotions* (Louisville: Westminster John Knox Press, 2007), 338.

3

QUIETING PRAYER

QUIETING, OR CENTERING and calming our thoughts, clears the way for our connection to Jesus the Healer and to our stories of His presence. But this is difficult, as much of life is high-alert, scattered drama—hardly conducive to the "steeping our souls in the beauty of the mysterious" that Abbott Delatte claimed is essential to our very survival.[11]

Buddhist-type meditative mindfulness is now a popular trend, offering to improve our work-life balance, cure our pain, settle our distress, and even halt our aging process. Those now in their 20's and 30's have been called "the Meditation Generation,"[12] flocking to this 'new' gym membership of the mind. But meditation is not new for Christians. It's been built into our creation purposes. We are commanded to share in God's rest (Genesis 2:2-3), to cease striving and acknowledge Him (Psalm 46:10), to listen in His holy silence (Habakkuk 2:20). Without this quieting connection, life becomes joyless and aimless (Exodus 33: 14, 15). In Matthew 11, Jesus clarifies this ancient prescription as being all about connection to

41

Him: "Come to Me...I'll show you how to take a real rest. Walk with me and work with me—watch how I do it. Learn the unforced rhythms of grace. I won't lay anything heavy or ill-fitting on you. Keep company with Me and you'll learn to live freely and rightly" (Matthew 11:29-30, The Message).

Biblical quieting calls us way beyond mental stress management to rhythms of trusting friendship that merge into practical, visible, life-changing behaviors. Quieting in His friendship stills our inner turmoil, rushing thoughts, crippling bodily tensions, and best-formed coping strategies. In quieting with hundreds of people, not one person has encountered a judging, frightening Jesus. In quieting, we come broken and needy, but to a Friend.

Jesus wants to heal us by sitting with us in our trauma. If pain surfaces, He wants to heal us, not judge us (James 1:2). The pain may even get worse as we are honest with Jesus about our brokenness. As Susan discovered, this can dredge up feelings of vulnerability and even shame:

> I can't ask for the presence of Jesus because I'll fall in a hole. I've been abandoned many times. I've always feared loneliness and expect that one day I will be lonely again. That came true in my first relationship. So I decided I would make people need me to get love so that no one would ever hurt me again. I've been really successful in keeping my guard up, then someone got under my guard and hurt me. I wasn't prepared for this. Now I can't deal with the pain.

Smoking helps, wraps it all up and makes my heart cold, less open...but at least I can survive. I feel stronger—a false confidence, I know, but I am in a zone where no one can hurt me. When I give up smoking I'm gentler, open-hearted, better able to relate, and more empathetic. But my heart feels full of mush because I feel weak and out of control. Of course I don't like to show this part of myself. Quiet is very hard for me.

We held her "ball of mush" quietly and gently in the healing presence of Jesus. This is the very space where Jesus wanted Susan to sit with Him: in her mush, out of control, defenseless enough to discover His presence in the quiet assurance of His acceptance. No words were necessary. Eventually peace came, so we could proceed.

Quieting calms our insistent pain stories so that we can find stories that contain healing seeds underneath. Jesus has uniquely and personally crafted these healing-seed stories for renewed life with Him. Quieting also liberates the prayer leader from the impulse to solve, rush, advise, or supply images for the person. Together we welcome the presence of Jesus and wait, joyfully attentive to what He will say or do.

Quieting to Open a Prayer Session

AFTER OPENING the session with a simple prayer, anointing with oil, and sometimes communion, we prepare for quieting by asking, "What do you appreciate or like about Jesus? What do you find relevant about Him to your situation now?' It is important to personalize this, not borrow a cliché or use a general statement. This appreciation of God's character may come from a favorite Bible verse, a story, an experience in nature, or a person who is a reminder of Jesus.

We say the words of this simple prayer while the person focuses on meeting Jesus. For example, the person may choose, "Jesus, You are my strength," from Psalm 73:26. So we say:

Thank You, Jesus (as the person breathes in deeply and we pause for 2-3 seconds)

You are my strength (the person breathes out fully and slowly)

We practice this several times until they have a sense of Jesus near, with His peace settling them in the time. Jesus becomes their incarnational reality. The focus shifts from their mental and emotional turmoil or any physical pain, as they make an effort to breathe deeply.

Most people are able to connect to Jesus through this kind of simple quieting. Sometimes we need to do it several more times. We ask permission to stand at their side and place one hand on their forehead and the other at the base of the back of the head. This is intended as a comforting gesture that assures them that they are not alone and can find relief from their tension to focus on Jesus. Other times, people present their pain to Jesus with open palms, and we place our hands on theirs as a symbol of His healing covering. Then they are able to continue to encounter Jesus as a friend and companion in their healing story.

Returning to Quiet

QUIETING PRAYER BEGINS the prayer process, but it also opens up and confirms each step. Stella's story is particularly illustrative. She came to us with a huge amount of anxiety about many things, including whether to pursue academic or ministry training. She told us about a long-time anxiety disorder that caused her to pull out her hair.

As is often the case with those who have high anxiety, quieting seemed like a real challenge for Stella at first. Her first choice for quieting was, "Thank you, Jesus. You are my friend." When she expressed frustration with the busyness of her mind, we encouraged her to repeat her concerns to Jesus.

"Jesus, why is it so hard to quiet?" she asked. A few moments later, she told us, "I'm not sure it's an answer to my question, but I sensed his reassuring me that I don't have to do everything by myself." Clearly He did answer her question—quieting is not another task to accomplish. It's connecting to Jesus. So we came to Him again with, "Thank you, Jesus. I don't have to do everything myself." This cleared the way for her to remember a joy story that reminded Stella that He lives in and with her.

Her next response was honest: "I know this in my head, but I don't feel it in my heart. What I hear is condemnation. It's a struggle. God sees my body, but I'm failing to make my body hospitable for Him. I have the gift of physical beauty, but I ruin this by pulling my hair out. Maybe we should quiet again on Jesus' promise that He lives in me."

So we did: "Thank you, Jesus. You live in me."

"That's hard to accept, but quieting definitely makes me lighter and less weighed down," she said. Stella was ready to tell her pain story. She shared that in a violent household, she became the protector of her three younger siblings at an early age. Sometimes she hid in the bathroom and read for hours to escape. She was lonely at school too, being both a racial minority (Black/Bengali) and very bright. This was the context in which she started pulling out her hair at the age of six—twenty-one years ago. "It's now automatic, painless, gives me relief from stress—but it makes me unhappy...I think I need to quiet again," she concluded.

So we returned to, "Thank you Jesus. I don't have to do everything myself."

At the end of the session, she shared, "I know the Lord is doing something. I worry when it's slow and doesn't seem to be working. I get distracted by attacks on myself. But in quieting, I do get some joy that good things are happening, some clarity about those attacks."

Alternative Quieting Scripts

Quieting On Our Loved Ones

What happens if people can't connect at all to Jesus in quieting prayer? Not everyone we meet with is a church-goer, and some have in fact had very damaging experiences in religion, but we assume that everyone is on their way to Jesus. In these cases, we try an oblique approach to Jesus through an appreciation story. We ask, "Who do you really appreciate? Who believes in you, accepts you?" Any appreciation story can lead more naturally into quieting prayer.

The person Janet appreciated was her grandmother. "I can't go straight to Jesus, but I can go straight to Nan," she said. "My parents were closed off, but once a year I'd visit Nan and she'd take me to the shop, buy me something, and ask the assistant to put it on her account. I loved that. I got my favorite outfit on Nan's account, though my father then refused to let me wear it. Nan just wanted to treat me, to bring out the best in me. I still hear her saying, 'Put it on my account!'" We affirmed that her delight over her grandmother's generous love was a link to the extravagant affection of Jesus. We quieted, focusing on, "Thank You Jesus. I am generously loved." We did this over and over until peace was restored.

For another person struggling with isolating addictions, we shared stories about his Grandma, laughed at some of his childhood escapades, and he became less agitated. Lingering over Grandma's beauty, kindness, and acceptance, he began to see something of Jesus in Grandma (he knew much more about Grandma than about Jesus). Eventually he didn't want to stop. "I'm enjoying this. Why isn't church like this?"

Relating appreciation stories is the main prompt for quieting in joy groups. As each story freely tumbles out, we ask, "What message about yourself do you get from this person who appreciates you? Finish this sentence: I am..." Readily people respond: I am appreciated, worthy of good, not forgotten, loved even when I'm revolting, listened to, and more. Then we communally quiet, using each person's response: "Thank You Jesus. Lisa is accepted even when she is revolting." "Thank you Jesus. Ben is worthy of good."

Quieting like this is evangelizing—connecting people to the Jesus who is longing to connect to needy people. It also connects people to others, and surprisingly, to their own true hearts. Quieting also leads to repenting. The tenderness of the presence of Jesus overwhelms resistance to His grace. This happens over and over again. Quieting into repenting lays a deep foundation for healing.

Quieting for Body Healing

The presence of Jesus in quieting prayer releases us from having to ask for any particular form of healing. Often physical healing freely flows in His presence, especially if physical pain hinders the quieting. "My chest hurts when I try to quiet," said one lady, "There's so much pain there." Slow, gentle breathing with quieting gradually releases pain. Our every breath is a gift from our Creator (Job 23:7), and we have seen that deepening our breathing while quieting draws more of His Spirit into our broken bodies, souls, and spirits.

Jesus makes the connections to that which we have forgotten or locked away in order to stop remembering. Our bodies remember and truthfully express the severity of the pain in our stories.[13] Physical pain can be present for a number of reasons. At times pain can indicate demonic interference, similar to what is seen in stories recounted in the Gospel of Mark (1:30-34; 5:1-13; 9:14-29). Whatever its cause, pain guides us to what Jesus wants to do right now and we follow His leading.

A prayerful body scan often locates the area and the source of pain which Jesus wants to heal. We ask Jesus to come to every part of the person's body—from top to toe. If pain emerges at any part, we quiet with Jesus as He heals what is located there.

Extended Quieting on a Story

When the person shares their story of the presence of Jesus, we go over all the details, slowly, in guided prayer. This honors the story and celebrates the healing discoveries in the presence of Jesus. We once had a session with Marta, who was convinced that she had no voice. She withdrew into the idea that she is not cherished, always caring for others but never for herself.

Had she ever been touched by the presence of Jesus? Yes. She immediately thought of a funeral that she attended years ago in a beautiful garden. As her three young children played quietly, a man from a previous service approached her and spoke of his fear of death. Without any hesitation, Marta told him of Jesus' love, and to her surprise he was open to accepting Jesus as his Savior. An amazing, deeply moving healing moment followed as she cried, "God uses me in my weakness."

Slowly, securely, gently, George recounted all the details of the story, the beauty, the surprise, all the colors, emotions, as Marta quieted and revisited her story. Out of this emerged new insights—about Jesus and about Marta herself. So encouraging, so connecting to Jesus.

Quieting Without Words

In the presence of Jesus, words are often not necessary for quieting. We saw this in one beautiful healing prayer session in a very poor South African township. The couple were newly married and came together for healing prayer. Their wedding photos were filled with exuberant dancing. This young wife from a very distant place was now serving her husband's extended slum household of at least nine dependent relatives—all women and often ill. When asked what they appreciated about Jesus, the beautiful young bride simply cried, "I must kneel before Jesus." Holy awe filled the silence that enveloped us. Her care-worn face softened in the flow of speechless worship. What was happening? Was she finding the resources to face a seemingly impossible future together? We were not sure what was happening, but we knew that Jesus was present to heal us all. In place of words and breakthroughs, Jesus offers us His incomprehensible presence—no solutions, no insights, just Himself, our "I am."

From this lovely young bride, we discovered the essence of quieting in prayer ministry. It's such a relief not to need the right words, the right questions—just gently connect people to Jesus. We're still learning to trust the healing power of His wordless presence. Even Elijah expected to meet God in powerful words, earthquake, or fire, rather than in gentle whisper—literally, *a sound of gentle stillness* (1 Kings 19:12).

Quieting for another's healing is only as effective as our own quieting with Jesus. Shamefully, I once found myself fishing for some personal credit for a person's healing when I asked, "At what point did you experience healing?" The answer was the corrective I needed: "Most healing has come when there was no talking, in the quiet, the ordinary, just being together. You just waited me out. That's healing, as my whole life has been about some-one forcing, pushing, wanting me to be someone, or be somewhere else."

This reminded me of a comment from a woman recently widowed after a happy marriage: "I have plenty of peo-ple to do things with, but nobody to do nothing with." Resting, quieting with one another and with Jesus, is the optimum healing, loving place. We give up our doing to quietly do nothing in His presence. Then He gives us His everything.

A Lifestyle of Quieting

We practice quieting in prayer sessions not just to make way for our storying time, but in hope that the person will incorporate quieting into the rhythms of their life. Quieting becomes so natural, so healing, when it is prac-ticed regularly. Favorite music and photos help access quieting. We can quiet anywhere, at any time. In the car, supermarket, in an argument, a business meeting— there is no place that we can't connect to Jesus in our spirits. Technology, too, can help. One young man even wanted his extended quieting recorded on his iPhone. Now he can play it, re-enter this peaceful place, when his addiction rages.

Our daily lives demand the quiet focus on Jesus as mod-eled in our LIFE sessions. Sharon, a friend who is slowly processing deep trauma related to childhood abuse, told us, "When I'm terribly confused, I quiet—it's like taking a mental nap, putting the negative thoughts to rest so that I can see and act clearly, rather than just retaliating against the abuse."

We can train ourselves to develop a lifestyle of quieting in the presence of Jesus: more focus, more being present with Him. Many times a day I pray the Lord's Prayer to quiet any negative thoughts. Often I'm distracted, so I start again, marking each phrase on my fingers until I am focused on His Kingdom, His power, His glory. The quieter I become, the more I can hear God's longing to quiet me with His love (Zephaniah 3:17).

Quieting Is Better Together

Quieting with safe others builds confidence and overcomes isolation. We remember that healing is all about connecting—with Jesus, others, and ourselves. George and I do this as a tender, united way to celebrate the precious gift of a new day with Jesus and each other. We hold each other, synchronize our breathing, and George says as we breathe in and out slowly: "Thank You, Jesus. You are with us." We follow this with scripture reading and communion. Such precious unity together with Jesus.

Quieting, too, transforms casual sharing with friends. When a friend shares a problem, we can honestly admit, "I don't know how to advise you, but we can quiet together in the presence of Jesus to listen to what He will say or do." Advice-giving (even if it is very sound) may prevent the person in pain from learning to go straight to Jesus in those dark night hours when no friend is nearby. As friends we are freed from being problem solvers to admitting our mutual need for the presence of Jesus to transform us into companions of one another's joy (2 Corinthians 1:24). What a relief that is!

Activities for Application

1. What do you appreciate about Jesus today? Turn it into a quieting prayer.

   "Thank you, Jesus" (hold for 2-3 seconds)

   "You are my peace, joy, friend, etc..." (release)

   Do this until peace comes. Make it a daily habit, and keep a journal of your quieting prayers, noting the changes you see.

2. In your scripture reading, respond with personalized quieting prayers. Say them slowly at least 5 times each so that they become part of your whole being. This is a sure resource for healing and maintaining healing. Examples include:

   Thank You, God. You make everything beautiful in its time. (Ecclesiastes 3:11)

   Thank You, Lord. You turn my darkness into light. (2 Samuel 22:9)

   Thank You, Jesus. You won't let things around me squeeze my life away. (Romans 12:2)

3. Ask a partner if you could guide them in quieting prayer. This may be a person in obvious need of peace, or simply

a person who is willing to explore something new with you. Enjoy some time together, then ask your friend what they appreciate about Jesus right now. Articulate the prayer for them as they focus on Jesus and accompany this with slow, deep breathing. Share your experiences.

[11] Abbott Delatte, as quoted in Evelyn Underhill, *Light of Christ: Addresses Given at the House of Retreat Pleshey, in May 1932* (Eugene: Wipf and Stock, 2004), 105. Abbott Delatte was a French Benedictine monk who lived from 1890 to 1921.
[12] "The Meditation Generation," *The Australian*, September 12, 2013.
[13] This is often called psychosomatic (mental-physical) pain.

PART TWO:

IDENTIFY PAST STORIES
OF HIS PRESENCE

4

A STORY APPROACH TO HEALING

OUR FOCUS ON STORY in the CompanionLIFE rhythm is quite intentional. Healing is connecting to Jesus, and remembering our stories of His presence can help us to do that in a unique and powerful way.

Safety is essential for healing. Relational, gentle story-telling can provide that safety. Neuroscientist Dan Siegel adds that telling our stories helps us to be more flexible, adaptive, coherent, energized, and stable—all the features of an integrated brain.[14] Stories work perfectly with these needs of our brains, opening safe healing paths and empowering us to walk on them.

The old biblical word for "testimony" is related to the picture of a safe path,[15] a path of truth where we discover God's renewing presence, His unalterable promises. Our safe-path stories themselves are crafted by Jesus to take us straight to Him and to His fuller story. He is active in our ongoing stories, preparing us for His healing so we can recognize His touches of eternity right in our ordinary life events and even in times of great pain.

In our stories we discover that we have encountered Jesus many times before. We remember what we are like in the presence of Jesus. We remember how He sees and treats us. Knowing that our circumstances change, but He doesn't, we can be assured that He will treat us the same as He did in our story when we invite Jesus into our current pain. It's no wonder that stories are so precious to Jesus. As Madeleine L'Engle said, "Jesus was not a theologian. He was God who told stories."[16]

In Luke 24, the disciples on the road to Emmaus experienced this. After the devastation of Jesus' execution on the Cross, they descended into the worst interpretation of their stories: *"Jesus is dead. We're all cursed. It's over."* But Jesus joined them in their journey, an uninvited companion. He reminded them of their most-loved God stories—stories that showed how evil would be conquered, and life would come out of sacrifice. The seven-mile journey home became an encounter with a friend who, through stories, led them to His healing safety. This energizing re-encounter with their own stories of God's presence led to restored relationships and ongoing courageous mission. Healing always calls us beyond ourselves.

This story has been an amazing inspiration for us as we companion others in their own stories of Jesus' healing presence.

Centering on Story in Prayer Sessions

THE PREVIOUS SECTION walked through our usual rhythm for opening prayer sessions: acknowledging Jesus as the center of our sessions, building joy, and quieting on the aspect of Jesus that resonates with the person seeking healing. After building this healing capacity, it's time to relate stories of the presence of Jesus—actual examples of His presence in our lives. Remember we begin here, with accessible stories of Jesus' presence, rather than with the aching stories where He seemed to be absent. We present those urgent pain stories to Jesus for later healing care.

Prompting the Story

We have found that every person has experienced the presence of Jesus (see Romans 1:19). Even if His touch is fleeting, it is always beyond our initiating, beyond the boundaries of our theological comprehension. Of course this doesn't mean everyone would be able to answer a simple question asking, "Where has Jesus has shown up in your life?" Sometimes we do ask just exactly that, but some people (both Christians and non-Christians) need gentle prompts from photos, nature, music, online posts—any source that leads them to a story.

To train ourselves in gently asking for stories of the presence of Jesus, we can practice in ordinary life. For example, on one of my walks I approached a woman who was walking her dog. I admired the pet, and within a few minutes of conversing, she began to vent her frustrations about life in general and about her wayward son in particular. I noticed that she had a gold cross necklace, and I thought it might be a way to open up the conversation about her connection to Jesus. She told me that she loved her cross, and the tapestry of The Last Supper which hung on her wall at home, because they were treasures rescued in her escape from her war-torn home country. Her long story afforded plenty of examples of perseverance and courage for me to affirm. Could she ask the same Jesus from all of these stories, from her tapestry, to be with her in her son's chaos? A new thought, but a welcome one. We prayed together on the street.

A ready source for a story prompt is the person's chosen phrase for quieting. If they quieted on peace, we might ask for a story of a time when they experienced peace. In fact, sometimes these memories come back to the person spontaneously during prayer, and all we need to do is ask, "What came to you as we quieted?"

Claire came for prayer as she prepared to be married. She and her fiancé had committed to live and work in an urban poor community. Life, she said, was "good, but hard," a mixture of wedding joy and uncertain finances, with no guarantee of an extension of her teaching contract. She longed for Jesus' peace again, so we quieted on, "Thank you, Jesus, for your peace."

As she quieted, a "good, but hard" story came to her of a favorite difficult hike back home in Hawaii. Only at the end of the long hike could she see the beautiful view. Good, but hard—just like her current situation. Then we asked Jesus if there were other good, but hard stories He wanted to refresh in her memory. Several emerged, but we focused on her favorite one.

"It's about my dad. I miss him and I want him at my wedding. He died when I was seven. Ten years later, my finances were low and I was about to drop out of college. Surprisingly, I got a letter informing me that I would receive Dad's uncollected social security payments.

Enough money to finish college! I've never before realized how his love for me was active even after he died. I just put him in a box and so limited the power of his love and God's love to reach me."

Seeing the way her dad's love was still influencing her life was a comfort to Claire as she anticipated missing him at the wedding. It showed her that God's love, too, would stay with her and provide for her throughout an uncertain future.

For non-Christians, looking for Jesus in their lives can feel foreign or forced. We might instead ask, "Can you tell me a story of someone who appreciated you?" or "Do you have a story about a wonderful moment you didn't strive for or initiate?" We might then share that Jesus is just like what they experienced, and this can give them a point of connection.

Understandably, some people have trouble remembering beyond their current story of pain at all. A story of the presence of Jesus is so often the complete opposite of their pain story, so we might gently ask, "Do you remember a time when it wasn't like this?" or "When in your life have you felt appreciated, loved, seen—not neglected or abused?" If this type of prompting isn't effective, it may be helpful to spend some more time building joy before moving forward together.

Listening Together

The prayer leader (along with the companion, if present) comes as a listening friend, not a solver of problems. We resist the desire to tell our own stories, or to control the content or interpretation of what our friends are sharing. Our gentle, listening focus on the person aims to model the safe relational connections that are essential for the tender vulnerability of the prayer session.

This doesn't mean at all that our listening role is a passive or silent one. We are impressed with Jesus' questions in the Emmaus story (Luke 24:17-19). They teach us to help people develop their stories with obvious, patient questions like, "What happened?" "How was that for you?" "Say more." "Can you give me examples?" We acknowledge and affirm the person with our verbal and nonverbal responses: we lean in, we receive with gratitude, we enjoy the story with them, and we remain present to them.

Our LIFE aim is to establish a sense of what the person experienced of Jesus and also of themselves in their remembered story. Our two favorite interpretation questions are, "What were you like in the presence of Jesus?" and "How did He treat you?" Wonderful insights have emerged from these questions.

Re-Entering the Story

Retelling the story, pausing to quiet on every detail, often opens up fuller encounters with Jesus. More details emerge to reinforce the depth of His compassion.

If the person has brought a companion, we love to have them lead this form of extended quieting. During the retelling, the companion (or leader) checks for accuracy of the details and celebrates the heart of the person to have such a story. The retelling clarifies the way Jesus has worked previously and builds assurance that He can do this again.

Connecting to Now

As one person said, "As I hear my story again, I'm not focusing on the event details so much as on the person of Jesus and how He treated me. It's more about Jesus than my story." You can imagine our delight to hear this, as we recognize that this past-based connection with Jesus will help to carry her through her current pain. The dilemma is different, but Jesus is the same. It's on the basis of this reconnection with Jesus that we can pray, "Lord Jesus, come again into this current dilemma in the same way as You came before." This paves the way for the rest of the healing process.

Story Beyond the Session

WE HEAR STORIES all the time, and it's so natural to integrate healing principles into our casual listening. We've already seen an example of such a story encounter with the woman I met who was walking her dog. When stories just spill out of people, as they so often do, we can be prepared to prompt and listen for connections to Jesus' presence.

We can also invite stories in times when people don't expect to be known and deeply acknowledged. We Christians can become storytelling people, like Jesus and His ancestors. George and I do narrative prayer at altar calls, when hurting people come forward for healing at the end of a church service. Recently I was invited to pray for a young man who had been injured in a car accident. He was not at fault, but worries about back pain, insurance, and access to work spilled out as we spoke.

We quieted on his favorite thing about Jesus: "Thank You, Jesus, You give me peace." Then I asked if he had a story of Jesus' peace at another difficult time. He shared that when his family's house had burned down two years ago, he was amazingly able to help his parents care for so many complicated details. Recently graduated, he had no time or energy for a job search. But in the middle of this chaos he received two job offers when he hadn't even applied for anything! We asked Jesus to come again as He did in the fire story, now into a new pain and dilemma. Of course, this took a bit longer than just praying a quick blessing, but it gave the young man access to his own story-resources for remembering the presence of Jesus— something he could take with him for his continued healing journey beyond the altar call.

Story healing is not a quick-fix process. We've companioned people in their stories for years at a time. But that does not undervalue our smaller, temporary companionships along the way. One encounter, one everyday 'session,' can unlock healing, or change their pain trajectory just a little bit. We may never see what that person does with the seeds of healing they've discovered (see Chapter 6), but we can trust that any remembrance of Jesus will have meaning in their current lives. We now explore the importance of healing through remembering our stories, and inviting Jesus' presence to inhabit them.

Activities for Application

1. Tell a story from your life when you sensed the presence of Jesus. What were you like? How did He treat you?

2. Ask someone else to tell their story. Practice prompting questions, guiding questions, and the two reflective questions in activity 1.

3. Retell this (or another) person's story to them, slowly, thoughtfully. Reflect together on the experience of the re-telling.

---

[14] Curt Thompson, *Anatomy of the Soul: Surprising Connections between Neuroscience and Spiritual Practices That Can Transform Your Life and Relationships* (Wheaton: Tyndale, 2010), 162.

[15] Skip Moen, "God Repeats Himself," *Hebrew Word Study*, January 15, 2011, accessed November 12, 2016, *skipmoen.com/2011/01/god-repeats-himself.*

[16] Madeleine L'Engle, *Walking on Water: Reflections on Faith and Art* (Colorado Springs: Waterbrook Press, 2001).

5

REMEMBERING IS RE-ENCOUNTERING

THE LIFE HEALING PROCESS begins with joy building, quieting, and by inviting someone to recall a story of Jesus' presence, to meet Him both in their past and in their current challenges. This remembering is very biblical. We are created to remember (see Exodus 2:24 and Psalm 56:8), but most of us haven't developed this part of our design for healing.

Faith and memory are intricately linked. As Abraham Joshua Heschel, a 20th century leading Jewish theologian, said, "To believe is to remember."[17] This type of remembering makes our reflections startlingly relevant to our present experience of life. It re-presents an encounter with Jesus in a living story, not yet ended, inviting ongoing participation with His Holy Spirit. This is an actual encounter with the Eternal. When we draw on this faith encounter, we are not locked into the past tense, no mere doctrinal rehearsals. Jesus is present, available for our now, calling us to taste and see how His past goodness is ongoing.

Our call invites us to remember our own stories the way that God remembers us—tenderly, faithfully, mercifully, meaningfully. The request of the thief on the cross in Luke 23:42, "Lord, remember me when You come into Your kingdom," was far more than asking Jesus for a future mental note. It was a plea, asking Jesus to "act with Your promised grace and mercy towards me because I am placing myself under Your protection."[18]

Biblical remembering is an action word. When God remembers to do something, He restores and intervenes, based on His character (see Exodus 6:5). It follows that His "not remembering" our sins (Hosea 8:13) indicates that He will not act on what our circumstances deserve. But we are assured that He'll never have a memory lapse about His covenant promises to His people (Exodus 2:24), that they will be meaningfully acted upon in our own lives to this day.

Our human remembering, too, is active. It goes beyond just mentally recounting the details of God's work, says Anglican Benedictine monk Gregory Dix.[19] Remembering is a springboard for obedience-energized action. We approach decisions securely when we align with these proper God-markers in the past. We re-enter our stories of the presence of Jesus as participants, not as observers or solution searchers.

Think of 1 Chronicles 16:8-13, when King David calls his people to never forget what God will never forget—His promises, His ancient covenant, and His generations of kindness. Abraham, Isaac, and Jacob are long since dead, but God's promises to David's people were still available years and years later. Again, they encountered their

Deliverer and recognized in their current life-challenging reality His warning and saving, similar mercies to those of their ancestors. Biblical remembering is the context for healing encounters, healing actions, healing decisions. No wonder King David's people responded by singing their hearts out!

Remembering is also repenting, returning after the deviation from God's goodness, usually with deep grief. "How could you forget My goodness?" God pleads with people again and again (e.g. Exodus 13:3, 8, 14-15). In all our years of prayer healing, we have never needed to ask any person to repent. When they are immersed in the miracle of remembered love in the presence of Jesus, repentance flows. Forgiveness is accepted and extended to others. This remembering-repenting-forgiving declares that our past has no longer any power over our present. There is no past-tense focus in this kind of remembering.

How the Brain Remembers

REMEMBERING FOR HEALING is no archaeological dig into our murky past or search for accurate details, reasons, or solutions. We all know remembering can be very tricky, and helping someone to recall past events can be problematic.

Pressuring people to remember Jesus can cause serious harm. Planting a false memory by suggesting or prompting specific details for people is a form of abuse, and we need to be careful not to do so unintentionally. Our trust that Jesus is involved in bringing people to the right story and recalling the right details for their current moment frees us from trying to control the story they tell us.

This includes releasing any efforts to police accuracy in storytelling. Certainly, grounding the remembered story in its place, date, details, or even suggesting a title is helpful here, but "it's more important that memory helps us define ourselves," confirms Dr. Martin Conway.[20] Being rightly related is more important than being right in the Hebrew view of truth.[21] It's about living the truth, and holding onto one another in the chaos of change and imperfection in our stories. We remember our stories to connect, to help us become more whole, to find out that our little lives matter—even eternally. So we listen to connect, to hear what the person has to tell us about their experience.

Companions in Remembering

MOST OF US NEED some help in building our capacity for healing remembering. Research confirms that listeners who pay attention and show emotional responsibility help storytellers in both the recall of facts and the discovery of meaning in past experiences. Even sad experiences tend to take on more meaning when recounted with others.[22]

A few specific patterns we often follow are included here:

Remember Together

The whole LIFE process recognizes that remembering for healing is best done together. We need one another to help us keep drawing on His ways, His character, living in His presence, celebrating. Then we re-member again into a healing community—affirming more deeply who we are and whose we are.

Remembering our stories together affirms those God-given reference points in our lives. If a person is able to bring their own companion to sessions, we ask them about some things they've done together. "Do you remember when?" moments are some of the most tender and joyful, reinforcing the belonging between them.

The leader also begins to gather memories with the person over multiple sessions. After we hear a story of the presence of Jesus, we can continually reference and celebrate that story. In our experience Jesus leads people to the very right story that demonstrates the resources they need for healing.

The same is true in joy groups, as members build one another's capacity for joyful memory. A new attendee named Bridget said she could remember nothing of Jesus' presence in her life. Later as she slept, the Spirit surreptitiously uncovered some of her joy-filled stories about being in a choir. At the next meeting, the group celebrated her singing encounters with Jesus. Bridget's remembering added to others' remembering has over time nurtured their community identity as the joy story people.

Remember the Ordinary

Sometimes the story we remember is so ordinary that the comprehensiveness of His presence eludes us; we perceive it as being so fragmented that we miss the continuity of His grace. As we embrace these bits and pieces in the presence of Jesus, our stories become more united—we become more whole.

Jesus Himself is always sanctifying the ordinary things of our story as instruments of healing reminders. Everyday eating and drinking becomes our chief channel of healing in the Church. The participation-based "remember me" of the communion celebration keeps us grounded in this. His presence in the ordinary relieves our striving to find an extraordinary story in order to recognize His presence.

We can comfort those who feel they are without a grand story of Jesus with these fragmented reminders. We are not reaching for big stories. They will become bigger as He becomes bigger.

Pray for Remembering

Remembering the presence of Jesus—how He has been active in our lives—is the work of the Holy Spirit in us (John 14:26). Our memory is being prompted by the One who is personally present with us as an advocate (1 John 2:1); this is safe healing-remembering, not remembering to be further traumatized by the past. We can safely pray as people remember their stories: "Come, Lord Jesus, protect and comfort us as You lead us to the story when we met You or sensed Your presence. We want to meet You again in a similar healing way in our present difficult context."

The anxiety around trying to remember is a frustrating potential block to remembering. Quieting prayer (see Chapter 3) in particular helps people to more readily access their story as they focus on Jesus, not on a feverish dig into their memory. The story emerging out of quieting prayer is a living story of their experience of Jesus.

Apologies Can Unlock Remembering

Remembering stories of the presence of Jesus often takes a miracle of love. Our pain is magnified by the unforgiving inquisitor lurking in the shadows of our hearts, and we need desperately to be freed to focus on Jesus' presence.

In prayer ministry, one way we've found that this "miracle of love" can become a reality is to offer an apology for all painful remembering. George did this with grace-filled healing effectiveness for Shelley, a high achiever and successful academic who came to us for prayer. Harsh on her body, she pursued extreme sports to keep slim and attractive for dating after her divorce. Repeatedly she felt blocked from professional advancement by colleagues who betrayed her. In love, too, she was frustrated, as she never got what she wanted from men. She only remembered their constant betrayals.

Tenderly George responded to all of this, "In the name of Jesus who loves you and died for you, and as a man, I apologize for the lack of love and acceptance you have experienced from men. You were created for love and meant for loving acceptance, and I want to assure you that you deserve to be loved."

Shelley's harshness started to melt and she asked George to repeat the apology, as no man had ever apologized to her. He repeated a longer apology and held her eyes in loving focus. Tearfully she admitted, "I also betrayed my husband." The awful story tumbled out to allow the forgiveness of Jesus to cover the memories of striving and deceit. She became soft and gentle and opened her life to remembering stories of Jesus.

Establish Rhythms of Remembering

Remembering Jesus can become a healing habit, an activity to delight in regularly. The psalmist David says it's the best medicine for anxious insomniacs who need to do something in the long dark hours, not just lie there and stew: "I'll go over what God had done, lay out on the table the ancient wonders; I'll ponder all the things You've accomplished, and give a long, loving look at Your acts" (Psalm 77:11, 12, The Message). "If I'm sleepless at midnight, I spend the hours in grateful reflection" (Psalm 63:6, The Message).

Remembering can be a daily practice, but also a pattern of seasonal rituals—birthday storytelling traditions, advent candles at Christmas, graduation celebrations, anniversary letters, and so on. Remembering also adds healing comfort in seasons of challenging transition, such as relocating to a new place, unplanned career shifts, or losses. We remember how God, our "I am," conquers the never-ending flux of time.

Create Memorials

To prompt their so easily clouded divine memories, Old Testament Jews were repeatedly instructed to wear something (like the tassels in Numbers 13:39) or do something (like the Passover Feast in Exodus 12:14). It is so easy for the immediate to overwhelm the transcendent. Tangible memorials help preserve this healing connection of the everyday with the mysterious, of grateful obeying with His always-presence. We encourage these memorials to be personally designed. One woman encountered Jesus

73

in her pain as she stood on a hill surrounded by daisies, so she planted a pot of these flowers. Another drew a picture of a well where he met Jesus. Another kept a toy helicopter to remember how Jesus was with her during a medical emergency.

The Old Testament celebrates body memorials, such as those of the bejeweled High Priest. For us, too, it is helpful to have wearable memorial signs of faith, like a chosen ring or bracelet. Missionaries with Servant Partners wear a black Tucum ring to constantly remind them of their calling to the poor, a tradition with a moving story of reconciliation behind it.[23] Memorials go way beyond a memory jog, to a refreshed embrace of our Lord and His people behind the memorial. Keep, protect, and defend in your heart all that God is saying, Moses advised. The Message translation makes these memorials even more personal: "Get them inside of you...talk about them...tie them on your hands and forehead...inscribe them on the doorposts of your home and on your city gates" (Deuteronomy 6:6-9).

It is a fight to maintain or remember the presence of Jesus as our top priority, our healing focus. Creating our own memorials can keep our attention on Jesus!

Remembering Through Pilgrimage

For many, remembering in a physical location is a courageous step towards healing and forgiveness. For almost 30 years, Lyn had never wanted to go back to the city where her father died of AIDS. When she heard how a missionary colleague went back to El Salvador to revisit places of deep horror, she said, "If he can do it, I can. I need to go back there, to make a pilgrimage." She had always feared an oppressive place where all the horrible experiences would overwhelm again. She imagined everything would be exactly as it was 29 years ago, as if no time had passed, and she would experience the same level of trauma.

Yet Lyn knew that she now had more healing resources. She was going back as a different person, so the weight of remembering would not now crush her. The sacred journey with Jesus of pilgrimage was now possible, though not her natural choice. "I couldn't go back too raw," Lyn reflected. "This time I'm going back with Jesus because I am sure now I will find Him in those dark places."

She was amazed that after years of incarnational ministry in poor communities, she had only now understood that for her, too, darkness had a physical location. A place had become a tool of darkness and a hindrance to healing. She was used to calling others to enter into their darkness with Jesus, but she now took intentional steps to enter the physical place of her own remembered pain. As she did, she experienced Jesus' presence, was able to grieve, and that pain was replaced with Jesus' love.

Re-Encountering, Not Managing

According to recent research, remembering past events and imagining possible futures engage the same regions of the brain.[24] But a pain focus gets in the way of this energizing link! In sharing with a friend, I was really boasting that I did a lot of reflecting on my past. Her taut reply was, "But it's done you no good. You're still stuck." It was true—my remembering focused on my past pain and prevented my discovery of new possibilities through the challenges. Confronted, I knew I needed a more healing, releasing type of remembering.

Remembering to re-encounter Jesus allows Him to tear down the walls that protect our old chaos from His healing re-interpretation. There are compulsive tracks back to horrible memories, but this is a hurtful way of remembering; it requires practice to learn to interrupt this process until it becomes a healing habit. Success is usually slower than we'd hoped, and it may take several weeks to retrain our brains to go directly to the presence of Jesus to process our old pain.

Janet and I experimented with remembering Zephaniah 3:17 every day for six weeks to break a particularly distressing thought habit. Each day we focused on a part of the verse and asked Jesus to show us its relevance to thoughts and events, such as, "You are present right now," "You do the fighting today," "You calm me with Your love right now," and "You sing songs over me." She loves to sing, so choosing a song she would enjoy hearing from Jesus was very healing. We recorded and shared our multiple experiences of His presence. Remembering for healing still needs to be practiced so it becomes daily automatic habit.

Remembering the stories of His presence is inviting Him to drain the poison out of that bad memory that continues to haunt us. Sometimes it's immediate, or seems to be. Mostly it's a process—a lifelong process of remembering not to find solutions or comfort, but to intentionally re-encounter Jesus and His healing.

Activities for Application

1. Remember your joy story from Chapter 4. Create or find a memento (a piece of art, a stone, a poem) that you will see repeatedly and perhaps even carry with you. How does this help you connect to the presence of Jesus?

2. Draw a representation of your story and ask Jesus to accompany you to show you signs of His presence. Be surprised at all He reminds you of.

3. During the next birthday or anniversary party you attend, initiate a remembering session. For example:

    a. Ask the person to share a story from each decade of their life.
    b. Create poems, art pieces, and songs to celebrate the story of the person.
    c. Share old photos and reflect on the grace of Jesus pictured there.

[17] Abraham Joshua Heschel, *Man Is Not Alone* (New York: Farrar, Straus, and Giroux, 1976).

[18] Skip Moen, "A Thief's Theology," *Hebrew Word Study*, November 3, 2005, accessed November 12, 2016, *skipmoen.com/2005/11/a-thiefs-theology*.

[19] Gregory Dix, *The Shape of Liturgy* (London: Dacre Press, 1945), 161.

[20] Martin Conway, as quoted in "Current Research on Memory," *The Australian*, August 1, 2016. Dr. Martin Conway is Head of Psychology at City University, London.

[21] Skip Moen, "Says Who?" *Hebrew Word Study*, *skipmoen.com/2016/07/says-who*.

[22] "Current Research on Memory," *The Australian*, August 1, 2016.

[23] This story is told in various places. One online source is as follows: Hilary, "August Prayer Letter," *Word Made Flesh*, August 1, 2011, accessed November 12, 2016, *WordMadeFlesh.org/August-Prayer-Letter-5*.

[24] Daniel Schacter, "Remembering the Past to Imagine the Future: The Prospective Brain," *Nature Reviews Neuroscience 8* (2007): 657-661.

6

SEEDS OF HEALING

IT HAS BEEN A WONDERFUL discovery that any experience of Jesus' presence in a person's past story can become a seed of healing for their current pain.

Sometimes we hope, indeed expect, that a simple repetition of past positive events will bring us healing. When this doesn't happen, we feel bereft, a long way from healing. Now we are learning that the signs of Jesus' presence, His healing seeds, offer us a sure invitation to His redemptive reshaping of the pain-filled chaos in our stories.

Sue came to a prayer healing session with dashed hope. On her way, she was thinking of a near-freeway accident years ago. She avoided a crash then, but recently had crashed into a messy divorce. Protected then... why not now? What sense could she make of this disconnection in her stories? Both events were unwanted, with some personal fault. As we prayed, Sue discovered the connecting healing seed: Jesus had not left her alone, either then or now. A deep plunging into His healing presence proved to her that crash or no crash, Jesus was present in the confusion of her life.

As for Sue, the seeds of healing in our stories are the signs of the very presence of Jesus. In the unexpected, unwanted twists in our stories, tangible signs of these healing seeds can be unearthed. Even a tiny glimpse of His presence, no matter how blurry or forgotten, can be a healing seed. We call this a healing seed because any encounter with Jesus has the potential to regenerate and energize our ongoing healing and to link us to His imperishable seed, His very Word (1 Peter 2:23).

These healing seeds in our stories are personally and divinely crafted. They are as varied as the mysteries of our encounters with our Creator, our Healer. And yet, as we've reflected on the valuable contribution of Christian neuroscientists, we have discovered that these healing seeds respond to the basic questions all of our brains ask in the challenge of processing our pain. These questions, in order, are:

1. Do I belong?

2. Am I safe?

3. Am I stuck?

4. Am I growing?

5. Am I living from my true center?

These questions are our short adaptation of Karl Lehman and Jim Wilder's insights into the God-created plasticity of our brain and its discernible pathway to process our pain.[25] In every experience we ask these basic questions—in a millisecond, without cognitive input—in the fast-track (right side) of our brains. If these questions are not answered satisfactorily at any stage, our pain is not fully processed or resolved. Then, in the slower (left) side of our brains, we make a pain-based decision about this experience—for Sue, it was, "No one will ever protect me." Our healing journey is halted by this pain conclusion.

The transforming encouragement of brain science is that we are not destined to live in unprocessed pain. Jesus has planted the seeds of responses to our unanswered questions to make a way for healing. In His presence, belonging, safety, freedom, maturity, and life purpose can be found, nurtured, and grown to fruition.

Nurturing Seeds

IN PRAYER HEALING, the questions along the pain processing pathway are not asked overtly, but Deficit Cries (see Appendix C) in the person's story help us to look for the healing seeds that are most needed. Some of these signals and seeds are more intuitive than others. But it is critical to remember that these questions are not solved by stating the correct, theologically sound answers to them. Signs of Jesus' presence will unearth these healing seeds, and exercises will help to nurture them.

Belonging issues (Question 1) in particular are so foundational that they will probably need to be addressed over and over, even though we are growing well and finding our true purposes in God's kingdom. This was true of Carol, a missionary who was distressed again about visiting her estranged alcoholic father who claimed to now be a Christian. In prayer, she remembered two photos of her mostly absent father— rare photos of them together, both smiling, enjoying each other's company. Even though the photos had since been lost, remembering them unearthed a belonging seed where there was such an aching childhood deficit before.

Once seeds are discovered, they need to be nurtured so that their healing, life-giving potential is developed as fully as possible. This is why we explore stories with healing seeds in great detail. We give each story a name, an approximate or exact date, and a place.

We ask questions that draw the focus to the seed of healing, such as, "What were you like in this story?" and "What was Jesus like?" We ask companions or other group members, "What are you discovering about this person through their story?" "What are you discovering about Jesus?" We tell the story back to the person, usually as an extended quieting, during which the person closes their eyes and reconnects to Jesus in their story. Sometimes the person will write down, draw, sing, or act out their story. We fill out certificates to mark the discovery of healing seeds.[26] We don't move on too quickly.

A disturbing feature of the process is that words of advice are only helpful for discovering and nurturing seeds at the last level (Question 5), where the healing focus is on living from your true center, your full identity. Hence the caution to not give advice or answers. Instead we ask questions, return constantly to Jesus, and even withhold any prophecies until the person hears the message directly from Jesus. This synchronizing in the presence of Jesus is very healing and freeing for the person seeking healing and the companion.

Healing seeds can be nurtured and spring to life, even in the most unfavorable environment. We keep in mind that

Jesus was also called a "root out of dry ground" (Isaiah 53:2); His pain, suffering, and rejection was the unlikely ground from which the life of the world grew again. We trust Jesus to navigate immense suffering in an individual's experience to make way for new growth, new life, and new hope that pain and trauma can be processed.

Connecting to Biblical Seeds

Discovering similar healing seeds in biblical stories spurs on growth. We ask, "Is there a biblical story that affirms your story? How does this put your story in a larger perspective? How does it celebrate your part in God's larger story?"

Not everyone is familiar with the Bible, so we might suggest a story or ask if they would like to hear a story similar to their own, paraphrased. In groups, we might act them out together.

Julie was frustrated that her healing after many years in the sex industry was not progressing quickly or smoothly. She felt stuck in feelings of being unworthy and feelings of shame (Question 2). In a prayer healing session, Julie was able to locate seeds of healing, seeds of relating even in her shame. One night at 2 a.m. she was stumbling along the road with no money, no protection. A taxi driver offered her a lift and asked for no money or sex. This stranger recognized her worth, empathized with her, and delivered her safely. This story gave her a glimpse that she was worthy, capable of relating without sex and receiving from others without shame.

To strengthen this healing seed, we acted out a story with a similar theme: the wedding feast story of Matthew

22:1-14. We assigned different roles to play the king and the elite guests who refused the fancy invitations. We acted out the part where the street guests were given new clothes for the party. Julie said, "These are my people—but now I'm in the King's clothes, not my usual gear." Remembering and embodying the notion that Jesus and others saw her in the clothes of the banquet guest, not of the sex worker, nurtured the seed that Julie had discovered with Jesus.

Tracking Themes Between Stories

Jesus has scattered the seeds of our healing throughout our many experiences. What may be hinted at in one story can be clarified and emphasized by its recurrence throughout multiple stories. Over time, we see the intersections, the development of awareness, and the longing and fulfillment of longing for answers to our five questions. Story-telling overcomes any attempt to label themes as coincidences, because they are so embracing, tangible, even overwhelming.

This was true for Wendy, who expressed that she felt some hesitance around following a new calling into prayer ministry (Question 5). When she was asked if she had a story of the presence of Jesus in her life, particularly related to developing confidence in her calling, she told this medley of related stories, all with the same theme:

> We had just bought our house in the capital city, having lived in a country town for twenty-five years. A small ad for palliative caregivers caught

my eye, so I cut it out and pinned it to my cork board. I had no idea what I would get involved in.

Four months later after joining a church, the pastor, who hardly knew me, gave me a letter and said, "I believe this is for you." It was from the same place asking for committed volunteers in their hospice. Such confirmation of where God wanted me to be.

I have the most beautiful memories of the privilege of being with men and women in those last days/hours of their lives, of Jesus' loving presence filling me with His peace to share. On one very special time I was called to sit through the night with a disturbed, unsettled lady. When the professor of palliative care came to see her, I went to leave the room so he could attend privately to his patient. This gracious professor said to me, the volunteer, "Please don't leave. You are doing more for this lady than I can do."

Jesus blessed me greatly with those few words—me, a mere volunteer. The professor had no idea that through that experience I had the confidence to approach a nursing home and ask if they would train me, which they did. At 58 years of age, my lifelong dream of becoming a nurse came true. God knew my heart's desire.

Wendy's source of confidence in her new calling was as close as her own story, her own experience. Wendy knew what it was like to be prompted and called into a ministry, and to draw on Jesus as her resource to meet every challenge once she arrived. She felt that same prompting now, and didn't need to worry that she would be without His resources or that she misrecognized her design. This is her true heart: to be with people in need in the presence of Jesus. Once nurtured, those seeds grew to empower her to process a whole new set of challenges in leading prayer ministry.

Healing seeds do emerge in our stories and the themes that connect them, but they are not always obvious. Patiently listening, referring people back to quieting, and asking for links between stories all help these themes to emerge even from jumbled stories. We have discovered that Jesus will patiently lead us to the very themes that open His deep resources of healing for each person. Then, and only then, do we have sufficient capacity to move toward our unresolved pain.

Activities for Application

1. Which of the five questions along the pain processing pathway resonate with you? Which question most needs to be filled in through the growth of healing seeds?

2. Tell a story related to these healing seeds. Share it with someone else, and celebrate it together.

3. In your conversations and groups this week, see if you can recognize gaps in someone's pain processing pathway. Ask them to tell a story where seeds to fill those gaps might be found.

---

[25] For more on this pathway, see Appendix C. For more information on the work of Karl Lehman and Jim Wilder, see their websites: *www.kclehman.com* and *www.lifemodel.org*.

[26] See *www.ServantPartnersPress.org/SeedsOfJoy*.

PART THREE:

FIND HIM IN THOSE MOMENTS
WHEN HE SEEMED ABSENT

7

MOVING TOWARD PAIN

TURNING TO THE MOMENTS in our stories where Jesus seemed to be absent is by far the hardest, most courageous part of the LIFE healing process. Just as remembering Jesus means re-encountering Him (see Chapter 5), we also re-encounter our pain through remembering. It's no wonder that one community therapy group for violent offenders in California's San Quentin prison goes by the name of "Sitting in the Fire." But leaders of that group explain why we must do it: "We face our pain one piece at a time until it slowly burns up. Then we become peacemakers, healed people who heal people."[27]

For us in the healing prayer process, moving toward pain is not sitting in a murderous fire, but connecting with Jesus in His cleansing, refining, healing fire (Revelation 2:19). We sit there long enough for Him to flood our pain with His presence. Too often we fear we'll meet a judgmental Jesus, or think we'll only reconnect with Him after we fixed up our pain. Sally's story confirms how she had met Jesus right inside her pain, really like sitting in a fire.

In one mission I was processing a lot of pain. I was spiritually dry; God was distant. I saw myself in a war-zone, my life broken. In my image of destruction, there was a footbridge over a river to a land of peace. I longed to be out of that war-zone, as healing hadn't been coming.

Then Jesus entered that scene. I said, "Let's go and get away." He didn't move. I was a bit confused because I thought He was there to do some healing. For me, that meant He should fix it, clear it up, or at least we should leave.

In the end He gently said, "I'm here. This is where I'm at. Sit with Me. If you go across that footbridge, you go alone. The choice is yours—to go alone. But My invitation is to sit with Me in this."

I was stunned that His invitation was to be with Him in the war-zone. His agenda was not to put it all together but to sit with me, to be with Him there. I found myself accepting this, saying, "As long as You're here, I'll stay."

We asked Sally how Jesus had treated her as they sat together. She told us, "He was gentle, not demanding, not accusing me of the consequences of my anger. He didn't even blame me for wanting to go over the bridge."

Another confirmation: in all our years of ministry, we haven't seen anyone encounter a harsh or judgmental

Jesus as they re-entered their pain. Jesus has shown Himself to be supremely gentle, even toward those people who bore some responsibility for the pain they experienced. We can assure people that their encounter with Jesus in their pain will be an overwhelmingly loving one. Spontaneous repentance has often flowed out of love, not fear.

As we companion others toward pain, it is important to note that if our own pain is triggered by hearing someone's story or praying with them, we should go to Jesus with that experience and ask Him for our own healing. Our ministry is not to collect the burdens of others, adding them to our own. We need to be ready to seek our own healing, to focus on the presence of Jesus, to replenish our own joy, and to receive prayer healing from others regularly.

Guiding Sessions Toward the Pain

We pace our sessions (or the series of sessions) so that we move toward past and present pain only after we have done significant joy building, quieting, and re-encountering Jesus in past stories. We do this until the person receiving prayer is able to sit in Jesus' presence and experience physical, spiritual, and emotional peace, while noting any deficits in the pain processing pathway (see previous chapter). There is no need to announce the arrival of the pain phase, or any other phase for that matter. Our sessions flow as usual conversations do—two people moving from topic to topic as they're comfortable and ready. The prayer leader simply keeps this LIFE rhythm in mind, and may ask simple conversational questions that move the person back or forward along the process as needed.

There are varying responses to this third step of finding Him in those moments when He seemed absent. For some, the first two steps of the LIFE process—living in the presence of Jesus (joy building and quieting) and identifying past stories of His presence—mystically absorb their pain. As one person said after these two steps celebrated by communion, "That's all I need. I've connected to Jesus and I know how to continue to do this for my ongoing healing."

Another seldom but understandable response is impatience. "Why do we waste time on joy and quiet and not get on with healing my pain?" challenged one person. Healing for her was eliminating pain symptoms as quickly as possible. For some others, the fear of moving toward pain is crippling. "It'll be like a vacuum cleaner sucking stuff out of my life," despaired one individual. "The energy I need is astronomical. I'll only be paralyzed in pain, no motivation to go forward. How can I go to work?"

It is only with sufficient joy, quiet resources, and assurance of the presence of Jesus that we can move toward our pain. We are familiar with returning to our pain by simply recalling the hurtful memories, and it requires an intentional decision to alter that route—to face their pain in a new way. We affirm the courage and hard work of people who move toward their pain. We offer safe companionship at every step of the journey. The healing journey is a cooperative venture, and our part is to reconnect people to Jesus and His healing resources.

When it is time to move toward the pain, the individual will usually bring it up. If not, we may point them back to it: "Earlier today you told us you were experiencing _____. Are you ready to go there now?" We encourage people to say how bad it is, what it is like to have such pain. We don't need to know the details (especially violent and/or sexual details) of the pain, but we encourage people to walk toward it. We often ask how the person would like us to respond. Their requests vary from "just sit there," to "play music," to "hold my hand," and beyond. We remember always that God may not relieve the pain or change the circumstance, but He will establish His presence more surely inside the pain.

The next two chapters will discuss ways to partner with people in finding the roots of their pain, as well as knowing what to look for in the pain story once it's found. First, it's important to understand some basic principles for partnering with people as they begin to open up about past or present pain.

How Jesus Responds to Pain—
And How We Can Join Him

In all things, we look to Jesus as Healer. We want our presence, our sessions, to be about the same things His presence is about:

- Healing, not fixing
- Going deeper, not quicker
- Lingering, not escaping
- Relating, not demanding

Healing, Not Fixing

Fixing seeks a quick exit out of our pain—it's about patching up what is broken, maintaining control over the outcome, returning to our normal level of functioning as efficiently as possible.

Healing is about a genesis of wholeness—a new way of being. It is often complex, but our role is simple: to follow as Jesus takes control. Our healing question is the same as it was for the crippled man at the Bethesda pool: are we willing to do what is required to be made whole?[28]

Our focus on fixing ourselves never leads to healing. Anna came to us, saying, "Someday I'll get it all together and then be peaceful after all this suffering—when I'm thinner, married, more successful as a teacher and writer, and more fruitful in ministry. At 33, I'm too old to be dealing with this insecurity. I should just get over it, as my mother used to tell me." But what God did in her was much better than her own attempts at fixing herself. Sitting in God's presence, she recounted a biblical story and then invited Jesus into her own:

> I have felt the joy of Jesus' presence when I read and prayed about the Prodigal Son story. My dad left when I was young, but then I felt the joy of the Father's embrace—so graceful, incredible, comforting. It silenced the usual noises in my head: you're stupid, ugly, safer in the dark.
>
> Just now a memory comes to me of our first official dance in junior high. A boy said to me, "I don't dance with dogs." I was shocked, horrified

that it was true, that I was ugly. But I didn't react—that's my safe way to deal with pain.

We asked Jesus to come into that deeply submerged pain. She pictured herself back at the dance, and this is what she saw:

> I was floating around trying to find Him after it happened, and then He came carrying His cross, asking me to give Him my rejection. His life was all about rejection, just like mine. Then another picture of Jesus came to me. He was an older brother with a big backpack, offering to carry my rejection. So freeing, so different from believing I'm too messy to redeem.

Healing is so different from fixing. Constantly we are amazed that Jesus comes with healing as we sit with Him in the fire. Just as God assures us all in Isaiah: "I will not cause pain without allowing something new to be born" (Isaiah 66:9, The Message).

Deeper, Not Quicker

Most people tell their minor pain stories first and only reluctantly go to their deeper pain stories. We patiently honor each story told to us as this encourages the story-teller to feel secure and pursue deeper stories for deeper healing. One person cried out that her pain was taking her "down 124 steps," and so we waited patiently while she built the capacity to go one step deeper, one step deeper, while Jesus did His slow work in her.

We had been praying with Adi for several months about the long-term satanic ritual abuse she had experienced.

Hers was an awful, unbelievably painful story—too hor-rific to relate here. She told us, "I don't have to search for painful memories. They are in my face and in my body all the time." Then this email came:

> Recently my whole life flew before my eyes on a six-hour car journey. In all the images that came to me, I was always bound up by thick tape, even over my mouth. George and Dorothy, you were there, not troubled like me—three of us in a circle with Jesus as He gently pulled off layer by layer of tape, slowly, painfully. Many layers fused together by years of pain.
>
> At one point, I pulled away, scared of expos-ing my nakedness underneath—I never show how I feel inside to anyone, all this guilt and self-loathing. But Jesus gently insisted, "Don't pull away. These have to come off. If I help you, it will be less painful." More layers—I screamed, you cried, George prayed. Then I realized this was my healing. A healing story embedded in each piece of tape.
>
> Dorothy, now I can see that you weren't so trouble-free as you appeared in my vision. Your tendency is to rush in to alleviate my pain or devise a quicker, easier way to get down under-neath the layers. Don't do that. It's my unpeeling story, my pain, my healing, my sitting in the fire long enough to encounter Jesus' healing.

It's a privilege to be corrected this way—a privilege to continue to sit in the fire with this gifted, though wounded, person. Anything secret or hidden will control us. It has been a long journey, but we know that what is buried will only come back in greater force, exactly when it is most unwanted. Instead, we desire the healing that gets into the deep places, even if the process is very slow.

Lingering, Not Escaping

Pain triggers are difficult topics or images that make a person wince in pain, make them reluctant to move forward. Lingering in the pain means following those persistent pain triggers, not avoiding them or explaining them away. We recognize them as signposts to a story of healing, a deeper encounter with Jesus. The following chapter will explore triggers in greater depth. The principle to remember is that we don't turn away or cover up the feeling produced by triggers with false coping strategies. We linger in the presence of Jesus.

Coping strategies may have been a temporary salvation in a time of crisis, in a time before knowing the close presence of Jesus. But now, in the safety of His presence and with replenished resources, we can do better. Although Jesus is here even when we feel as though we experience Him the least, jumping out of the pain to coping strategies only delays His healing presence. But even in our habitual coping strategies, He still comes and offers to sit with us, and Jesus always accepts any invitation to speak and act right inside the pain.

Often we sit in silence with people as they enter their pain. We know that people in great pain are usually called to places of deep faith that we have never visited. They are teaching us the mysteries of trust in their courageous lingering. We say, "Let's just stay here in the presence of Jesus as affirmed in your stories. Let's wait until He drains some of the poison out of your pain. Come, Lord Jesus."

Kate was a born in a poor country, and had recently become a missionary to another. Despite the external difficulties, her real pains were relational, triggered by a breakup with her coworker boyfriend. She shared,

> My boyfriend couldn't commit, so I lived under his threat of abandoning me for 4 months. Just now I realize that this pain echoes the anxiety of Mum's slow dying 13 years ago. It was also like living under the threat of abandonment, being left alone. Others, including Mum, pretended it wasn't happening. When she finally admitted she was dying, I hoped I'd have more time, because we'd never been close. Then two weeks before she died, she gave me an old ring and said she loved me. By this time, I was numb and disconnected. Already abandoned.

We asked if she was willing to sit with Jesus in this difficult memory. She said, "Yes, but the hospital room has those sterile bad smells of sickness and noisy machines; thinking about it overwhelms me. Just let me go outside for a while." Later, when Kate returned from her small escape, she was ready to accept the invitation to linger. While she was away, Jesus kept bringing to mind a sign of her mother's acceptance—that old ring. Could something good happen in the old hospital memory? She asked Jesus to meet her in the hospital, and He did, sitting with her in the hallway in the final hours of her mother's life. We prayed, "Thank you, Jesus. You are with me."

Kate later related the surprising relief of actually going to the pain—what she had always dreaded and at first avoided. Lingering seems impossible, but Jesus is always waiting to meet us in the pain.

Relating, Not Demanding

In sitting in the fire we come to find, though we often admit it reluctantly, that it's Jesus we really need—not instant deliverance, not justice, not apologies, not all the things we assumed would bring us healing.

The difficulty of meeting Jesus inside our pain often leads to the surprising, overwhelming delight that our responses matter so much to Him. He wants to relate to us, as Helen discovered. She came to us for help with her marriage, saying,

> My husband is locked in an emotional prison, hurting everyone around him. Daily I'm frustrated with him and God because nothing is changing. I have a horrible thought that I might have to live with him like this. I'd like to shake him until he wakes up. How do I get deliverance so that this pain doesn't touch me?

We asked Helen if she had ever known deliverance from pain. She told a story from her cancer journey. She described it as a time when no family could comfort her, all locked in their own pain prisons—especially her husband.

I was sitting by myself, talking to the Lord. His strong presence really comforted me, took away my fear of dying, pervaded every barrier with a bonding stronger than I have ever known with mother, dad, or my husband. I didn't have to be strong. I want to get back to this but it's elusive, so I will just have to get on. I miss this bonding.

As we waited with Jesus to come again in that same way, Helen could see that she was sharing the pain of the work He still longed to do. "Asking more of Jesus means admitting I am still in pain. My pain matters to Him. This brings me rest," she told us. Comfort was relational, not based on demanded solutions.

We have so much to learn from the suffering people of God about their sitting in a tangible and refining fire, but always finding Jesus there. Hundreds of current stories inspire us, like this one: Two Christian widows in a poor Asian community are barred from the government grant of a cow for each family because they won't renounce their Christian faith. They also endure fiery pressure from their angry families. "Aren't we worth more than a cow?" they demand. How would we respond? Then one Middle-Eastern pastor — also persecuted for his faith — finished the service with this benediction: "God is here, in the fire. Jesus is here. The Holy Spirit is here. We must stay together and love, love, love."[29] These faith-filled, suffering friends are showing us that whatever the ferocity of the fire, we can be assured that we will find Jesus there.

Activities for Application

1. Tell about a time you "sat in the fire" of your own pain or accompanied someone else in their fire. How did Jesus make His presence felt?

2. Which of the four principles of Jesus' presence (healing, not fixing; going deeper, not quicker; lingering, not escaping; relating, not demanding) have historically been the most difficult for you as you've counseled others in their pain?

3. When others share their pain with you this week, focus on listening. Stay with them in their pain. If appropriate, join them in asking Jesus what He wants to do or say in their pain.

---

[27] "Sitting in the Fire," *Insight-Out*, accessed November 1, 2016, *insight-out.org/index. php/trainings/89-sitting-in-the-fire*.

[28] Variation of John 5:6. See Skip Moen, "Do You Want To Be Well?" *Hebrew Word Study, February 9, 2009*, accessed November 13, 2016, *skipmoen.com/2009/02/ do-you-want-to-be-well*.

[29] Andrew White, *Faith under Fire* (Grand Rapids: Monarch Books, 2011), 57.

8

FINDING ROOTS OF PAIN

ONE OF THE HARDEST discoveries in life, and in prayer healing, is that old pain keeps resurfacing in new ways. The person seeking healing rarely connects their current pain to their old traumas, but neuroscience tells us that there is often a strong relationship between them.

Our current distress, however minor, can be amplified to an intense level of pain because we experience it as just the latest episode in a whole backstory of hurt. We may physically carry unresolved pain in our bodies. Small, ordinary things can remind us of stories we have chosen not to think about, sometimes making everyday life very painful. Finally, we operate and analyze our lives out of core beliefs that we developed when we were wounded—beliefs that might not be true or helpful.

Jesus always works underneath the symptoms, at the roots of things. He Himself was described as a "root out of dried ground" (Isaiah 53:21). His life on earth was like a tiny plant, emerging out of a hostile environment, with everything conspiring to keep Him weak and vulnerable to evil. Amazingly, His obedience and saving grew out of this fragile ordinariness because He chose to live in truth, not in any lies that this dried ground offered. This is so encouraging for us as we begin to discover the distorted bases and the shaky foundations of our pain—perverted understandings, actual lies we have been told or have told ourselves, and ingrained responses to hostile realities—all of which have become hindrances to righteous relationships, freedom, and joy in our lives. This understanding of roots gives us hope to find His truth-based healing, always soaked in the love that renews us, even in our messy life events.

Penny was constantly disappointed that her diligent scripture confessions barely penetrated the anger protecting her lonely heart. Further, her way-out-of-proportion responses concerned her and certainly did nothing for her struggling marriage. Frustrated, she came to us to trace her anger to deep roots of pain. After she built her capacities for joy with Jesus, we turned to that task, starting with her presenting problem:

> My husband is a busy person. He can't be still, can't be with me. He quite literally hides behind his newspaper. I hate that—I withdraw and get angry. Recently I pushed a table away when he didn't hear me. He responded like a stunned mullet, shocked at my actions.
>
> I've prayed so much about my anger and forgiven many times based on Ephesians 4:32 and Matthew 6:15. Then I think to myself, "Who do you think you are to be so important to be heard?" People only like me for what I do, not for who I

am. I'm an interruption, an encumbrance. I'm in the way again! I'm not worth the time.

We asked Penny if she had ever felt that way before.

Certainly. When I was about ten years old, my family moved from South Africa. I couldn't cope and I had nightmares. The teacher had no time for me in a big class, so I couldn't catch up. My father was too impatient to explain math to me. I concluded that I'm stupid.

Once when I couldn't understand a problem in class, the nun sent me to my brother's class (he was 3 years younger) to find out the answer and to come back and tell my class. The shame of this—the deep feeling of everyone thinking I'm stupid and no one helping me—was too much.

Now I realize that my anger for that teacher is like the anger I feel over my husband's paper. No one has time for me. I have to work so hard, way beyond my ability. I'm stupid, lonely, embarrassed, and not good enough. It's always like this. I'm angry at God too. I can see the patterns. So I'm still angry now.

We asked Jesus to come into this loneliness. She sensed that Jesus came to sit with her on the steps leading back from her brother's class. "He's taking the time to be with me, even if I can't do math," she told us.

Penny's current anger went way beyond the trigger of her husband's newspaper, way beyond even the embarrassments of years ago. Her pain was in the conclusions she made about herself, confirmed again and again: "No one is with me." This became her core belief, her truth. Jesus uncovered the root of her pain and applied His truth.

In the most important sense, we don't do any of this rooting out. Jesus leads. But Jesus is also gentle, not forcing where He is not invited. The session leader partners with the person in asking where we might invite Jesus—where in all the chaos and pain we might focus as a place to invite healing. To do that, it is helpful to understand pain triggers, embodied pain, and core beliefs.

Pain Triggers

OUR BRAINS CONNECT our experiences together in ways that we can't control. A woman can't eat runny eggs because they remind her of semen in her childhood sexual abuse. A man's dislike of dogs is traced to his mother's saying she preferred dogs to children thirty years ago. Listening to others share about a specific type of abuse triggers a minister's own unresolved pain. We can all cite times when uninvited yesterdays have invaded our todays.

We have learned that we must take note of these triggers—not to rationalize them away, but to bring them to Jesus for His healing unearthing. He allows stuff to rise up in order to heal us, not torment us. We encourage people to address triggers this way: "Jesus, here is my pain talking again. What do You want to show me?"

Quiet was a trigger for Ryan. We discovered this as soon as we began quieting prayer. He was able to articulate that being quiet or still made him feel like he was going to die. When we asked him to tell us more about this fear, he explained, "I have to super-exercise to prove to myself that I'm alive. I'm frightened if my heart misses a beat. Then I need to escape to a hiding place to get my breath back and hear my heart again. I run to still these fears, to keep my heart moving."

Why did quiet and stillness trigger a fear of death in Ryan? We prayed, and in the presence of Jesus he realized he had made a very early decision about himself: he was destined for death. He remembered coming to the scary conclusion after his siblings taunted him that he would die after he swallowed chlorine capsules. The insecurity of life followed him everywhere; only constant activity could cover it up. It took bravery and assurance from Jesus to move toward his trigger, to explore what came up in the quiet, and to invite Jesus to enter in and protect his heart, his life.

Embodied Pain

WE UNDERSTAND THAT our bodies often express the severity of our pain more truthfully than our minds admit. Greg, a church leader, came to pray for something that could be considered quite minor, but then he couldn't quiet. His right arm began to throb in pain. We encouraged him to ask Jesus what was happening. Disturbed, he told us, "My anger frightens me. I'm worried that I could lash out and hurt my wife and kids with this right arm. Is there some connection between my anger and my right arm?"

We waited silently in the presence of Jesus. After a while a school yard memory when he was eight became very clear. Returning to school after his beloved father's funeral, he lashed out at a kid who called him a bastard. It was such a forceful right swipe that he knocked the kid out. He was horrified with the thought that since he knocked a kid out with a punch, he might become a murderer. This early fear still surfaces at any slight annoyance in the home. He'd never made that link before, but the presence of Jesus was there to heal his murderous right arm and to comfort the heartbroken eight-year-old.

Core Beliefs

For both Ryan and Greg, and many others, triggered and embodied pain led us straight to a memory that was at the core of how they understood themselves. For many people, these "truths," or core beliefs, are a hodge-podge of fears, distorted messages, family expectations, take-away analogies, and haphazard popular maxims that never deliver.

I'm always going to be alone. Time should heal my wounds. To be male is to be dirty. Love is a lie. The people who expressed these false core beliefs are outwardly vibrant Christian leaders. These are not conscious or chosen thoughts, not attitude problems. They are not touched by words of advice, by attempting to make better choices, by self-discipline, or by biblical reprimands. They are rooted in deeply held experiences that must be revisited with Jesus.

This is why we invite Jesus into the strongest, usually earliest experience of this pain with its associated conclusion. We ask, "Is this true, Lord Jesus?"

A Gentle Uncovering

Our call in prayer ministry is not to hunt violently for roots of pain, but to invite people to tell any painful stories that the Holy Spirit brings to the surface in Jesus' presence so His truth can cast piercing, healing light on untruth. In this context, painfully untrue beliefs tumble out into comforting acceptance and cleansing.

The prospect of revealing and transforming falsehood at the core of our beliefs can be terrifying. As one person very directly told us, "For me, it's best to live in unreality, even a false safety based on striving, disconnection, and loneliness. That's what I know." Stories are good at revealing core beliefs because they get past these defenses to uncover our hearts. They provide a gentle way of embracing tender vulnerability. Theologian N. T. Wright puts it this way: "The best way to change one's worldview is through better stories."[30]

Jesus' spirit reveals and re-frames a person's core beliefs, without our effort, through His alternative stories. We experienced this with John, who quite literally unearthed a core belief that other people were always responsible for his pain, and that he had no role to play in any of the anger that was surfacing in his life.

> I've felt ripped off by lots of people. Then one day I took my frustrations out on an unruly vine covering my back fence. Ripping into it, I secretly blamed my neighbor for allowing his bad gardening to encroach onto my property. I slashed and tore at the vine for ages, only to discover that the root of the vine was on my side of the fence.

Immediately I realized that blaming others stopped my seeing some root issues in my life. I've tried to get my head around problems with others, ask for quick deliverance, confess positive statements and scriptures, but nothing changes. I've got to deal with some of my root issues, resolve some long-term pain that comes from always being ripped off, especially by my unloving father. I didn't cause it, but starting the healing process is my responsibility.

As is always the case, John did not need us to prod or coach a revelation in him. The Spirit sparked the epiphany that he needed to move forward. Gently, exactly as John could receive it in the moment, but so powerful.

Beyond Behaviors

Untrue core beliefs about who we are and who God is need to be transformed in order to bring healing. Changing outward behavior, rationally deciding on better choices, even excellent teaching of sound propositions—all of these are limited if personally held truths do not generate new life connections to Jesus. Usually we want to squash the troubling effects of bad behavior without dealing with the lies behind it. For all of us, the pervasiveness of lies in our lives is disturbing. What the reformer John Calvin said ages ago is still true: "The human mind is, so to speak, a perpetual forge of idols."[31]

Author John Eldridge agrees, "We will make an idol of anything—we are desperate for life, and we come to believe that we must arrange for it the best we can or no one will. God must thwart us to save us."[32] This divine thwarting exposes the undetected sickness of years living in lies rather than in truth. As prayer companions, we do not shield people from this devastation. We stay with them, immersed in the presence of Jesus, so they know that both Jesus and another person accepts them no matter what is uncovered about their "truth."

Urban missionaries know too well that lies are not just individual—they are comunal, corporate. And communal lies, such as racism and disparaging beliefs about those who are poor, lead directly to communal injustices. These missionaries do the slow, hidden work of rooting out these lies in their communities. There are so many parallels between personal and communal healing—all healing needs to come from the very roots.

Experience, Not Advice

THE TRUTH OF JESUS that dispels the lie at the basis of our pain must be experiential truth, not merely cognitive truth. We would never chastise Ryan for fearing death, insisting that he repeat back to us the neat truth about his eternal security. Healing must be personally relevant. It must connect people to Jesus, others, and themselves. This kind of truth is experienced in the presence of Jesus, where we discover what He thinks of us and how He treats us.

Everything that has led up to the part of the prayer session in which we deal with pain—joy building, quieting, stories of Jesus—has been put in place to build up resources for the person to seek Jesus personally. Even those who are low in biblical literacy have encountered and recognized Jesus in their own stories; they have experienced His truth and can invite Him into their pain, with or without us.

One highly trained professional chose to quiet with the words, "Thank You, Jesus, for Your sacrifice." Obviously a precious choice, but it seemed more academic or generic than personal. This is a common problem in prayer ministry with the theologically trained. But rather than judging or correcting this, we trusted Jesus to make Himself personally known to her. And He did. Now, after meeting Jesus in a hard story of deep loneliness, she is daily connecting to Him by quieting with the words, "Thank You, Jesus. I am not alone." Both prayers are equally true, but the new phrase will bring her back to her uniquely crafted personal encounter with Jesus.

No Straight Line

WHILE THE GENERAL ADVICE is to find healing in the earliest root of pain, the Holy Spirit guides us where He chooses. When Lee wrote a poem that traced her healing from rejection, she started at her present pain, moved to her teenage years, then to the recent birth of her child, then to her early childhood, and then back to the present. For her, this order held meaning, and she asked Jesus to enter into each incident along the same path.

Stories help us to trace the themes of people's pain processing. Their present trauma may look very different from their original pain, but with the same theme (e.g., rejection). We overlay that with the theme of their presence of Jesus stories (e.g., acceptance). We help people chart these events to discover that their times of greatest pain usually coincided with their times of experiencing most deeply the presence of Jesus. Such discoveries amaze and are very healing.

Patience for Persistent Pains

Often people have had lots of prayer and even therapy for a particular trauma, but have no idea that its effects are still reverberating through their pain-filled actions. This is not because prayer ministry is ineffective, but because there is an ongoing process of making deeper connections, of asking Jesus, "What is triggered here? What do you want to show me about my repeated unwanted responses?" Sometimes a person uncovers unforgiveness toward others or themselves; sometimes it is a different lie borne of the same pain that had gone undetected in past explorations. Every time our brains go back to the pain, there is an opportunity for further healing.

Thankfully, our persistent pain does not disqualify us from helping others to heal. Jill has an old, crippling pain that constantly triggered automatic self-loathing. Many times we have encouraged her to find Jesus in both her emotional and body pain and we've prayed about the roots, but the pain still surfaces on occasion. It is much deeper than we ever could understand.

The anniversary of the traumatic event associated with her pain was approaching. Would there be any release this time? Without consciously connecting to the particular date, we met for casual coffee just two days before. George thanked Jill for the privilege of joining her healing journey as companions. It was a tender moment.

Later, she mused over this sharing and sensed the Lord speak to her. She related, "With George's thank you to me, I moved from a focus on my horrific pain and guilt to a wider focus, a bigger picture of expanding joy for others. My way of embracing my forgiveness is to spread this healing to an outer perimeter. God is using my pain for the good of others. This is still hard but so releasing." Jill was encouraged that she had more freedom from her deeply rooted pain to draw on Jesus' love for others.

Activities for Application

1. Tell a story of when you discovered a root of your pain. How did this happen? What were the results?

2. Identify and discuss some of the examples of core beliefs in this chapter. Have you encountered any of them before? What effect have they had on your stories?

3. Pray with others about a current problem or trigger and ask Jesus about its roots. Invite Jesus to reflect on any words or come into any events that you remember.

---

[30] N.T. Wright, *The Challenge of Jesus* (London: SPCK, 2000).

[31] John Calvin, *Institutes, Book 1*, trans. Henry Beveridge (Edinburgh: Calvin Translation Society, 1845), 128.

[32] John Eldridge, *Desire* (Nashville: Thomas Nelson, 2007), 93.

9

HIDDEN SAPPHIRES IN STORIES OF PAIN

Early on in the LIFE process, we connected to Jesus through joy, quieting, and our past stories about Him. We trusted Him to sit with us in our stories of pain, and He has. But what about in traumatic past events themselves? Can we find this same Jesus inside of the black holes of our pain?

We've heard so many people crying out, "Where were/ are you, Lord? Why did You abandon me?" It is a life-shattering cry, and hauntingly consistent across the ages (Psalm 22:1; Ruth 1:13; Luke 15:34). We have all shared in this desperate plea to restore our relational connections to Jesus, others, and ourselves.

When that heart-cry is answered, when even decades later we can look back to a story with Jesus as He shows us that He did not abandon us, that story becomes sacred. We have seen this already: in Gus's story of realizing the gift of his daughter's short life (Chapter 1), Anna's invitation from Jesus to carry her middle-school rejection in His backpack (Chapter 7), and Penny's visit from Jesus on the steps during her painful walk back to class (Chapter 8). For each of these people, the encounter with Jesus in their pain became a shining, unbreakable proof that Jesus was with them and always would be.

One of my most delightful discoveries in exploring story healing has been to learn that the Hebrew word for "story" is related to the word for "sapphire."[33] Sapphires are one of the most precious, translucent, hardest gems, mined with great difficulty in the depths of the earth. Sapphires in the Bible always make sparkling divine connections, bringing far more healing than could have been imagined. Yet all the sapphire stories are in the context of great challenge, even darkest despair. These sapphire stories assure us that Jesus will show us something glimmering in the midst of our darkest hours too.

The Biblical Sapphires

What might Jesus show us when He enters our moments of deepest pain? A solution, a justification for the acts of an abuser, or a minimization of the trauma? No. Instead, He offers us a precious sapphire, a story about His presence. His healing presence in our pain stories reflects divine connections, similar to those in the biblical stories where this jewel appears. Here we mention six sapphire references.[34]

The Sapphire of Transforming Possibility (Exodus 24:10-11)

After dispirited wandering in the wilderness, Moses and the elders were actually invited to meet God. He was standing on a pavement of beautiful sapphires. Amazed by His overwhelming but approachable beauty, they feasted together from a peace offering. Not terrifying judgment, but intimate welcome. It was hope for a transformed relationship with their Covenant Keeper, sustaining intimacy on their puzzling wilderness journey.

In Sandra's wilderness marriage journey, she endured years of her husband's emotional abuse. The most painful recurring taunt was, "If only people knew you had an abortion as a teenager." Years of put-downs, rejection, and then divorce. But in prayer, she had a sapphire encounter. She met Jesus in the very room of her abortion, stretching His hand to shield all the condemning faces of her accusers. She wanted to hear Him say, "I forgive you." Instead she heard an even more encompassing statement from Him: "I love you." Life without guilt is the sapphire that Jesus holds out to her in her very own story.

The Sapphire of Tender Assurance (Exodus 28:18)

Another sapphire story comes from Aaron, the desert High Priest. A sapphire was one of the twelve precious gems on the breastplate he wore in tabernacle worship. When his displaced people saw the jewels, they were assured that their needs were continuously being tenderly presented, heard, and treated with honor in God's presence.

This was true for Robert, who was plagued with guilt over adultery despite lots of confessions. We waited in the presence of Jesus. What would He say about Robert's past? Then there was a tender sapphire moment. "What past?" Jesus asked.

The Sapphire of Deep Wisdom (Job 28:6, 16)

If our life is to sparkle with buried sapphires that have been found in deep ground, we must go deeper within our own buried stories. We must walk longer with God in our whole life's story to know His character and goodness to us within it. As Job contended with his accusers, surface scratching of God's ways doesn't solve the mystery of suffering. Quick answers slapped on to pain is still not the way of wise, healing companionship.

Sophie posed a Job-like challenge to us about our LIFE process: "Will you drive slowly over my speed bumps? Because I will feel every shudder of unwanted pain. Will you hold my head above water so I can begin to explore life without torment or secrecy? Do you understand that freedom will be harder, more foreign than being captured in pain?" We're thankful to Sophie for calling us deeper.

The Sapphire of Radiant Love (Song of Songs 5:14)

Often it's hard for us to accept the unconditional love of Jesus, especially when love is waning in our marriages. So Solomon's picture of the sapphire beauty of the lover's body seems excessive to the point of being embarrassing.

In healing prayer, wild, persistent love offers to break through our depressions and persistent negative self-talk. Shelley told us, "I was just staring at my work computer, almost paralyzed in the pain of my marriage separation. Then out of the blue the word 'advocate' came to me. I had to Google it to check the meaning. Advocate. Standing up for me. This is what Jesus is doing for me. Amazing after feeling so debilitated." Radiant sapphire love.

The Sapphire of Energizing Truth (Isaiah 54:11)

The questions for Isaiah's people was this: Could they rely on God's promise of a rebuilt sapphire foundation for their shattered lives? They were facing real terror, crippling sorrow, humiliating dependence on oppression. The lies that they believed about themselves and their future were overwhelming. Only God's truth could re-energize their healing journey.

God's sapphire truth still does this, as Peter discovered: "I only saw God through my Dad, always sending me into outer darkness without a word. Then Hebrews 12:2 hit me—removing my sin and blame gave Jesus joy. I feel silly that I'm just waking up to this at such a late age. But this strengthens me to go on."

The Sapphire of Hope for the Future (Ezekiel 1:26)

The world of the sixth century BC Jewish exiles in Babylon had fallen apart. Ezekiel the prophet offered them a hope that was impossible to see in their despair: a vision of God on His sapphire throne, promising later that their city would be renowned for His very presence ("God is there," says Ezekiel 48:35). Was God still sovereign in their chaos? Could He restore order? This truth was hard to grasp, but the sapphire vision gave glimpses of hope.

This same hope is an encouragement for urban missionaries working for justice against systemic corruption in their American cities. "It's step by step," says one leader at the apparent lack of progress. "But networks of hope between many different churches are developing as we support one another's dreams for cleaner, fairer cities."

Mining Together

Most of us find it difficult to see our sapphires alone. We have mulled over our pain story too many times to imagine finding something new there. Prayer leaders and companions can help to spot these gems in the muck of a hard story.

When people are wondering if there is any healing value in their stories, it is helpful to ask God, "Are there any sapphire signs of possibility, assurance, wisdom, love, faith, or future hope in my stories?"[35] We do not need to supply the answer, or pressure God for a quick one. Jesus will show them what He wants to show them.

Daniel came to us for individual prayer after finding a joy group that helped him begin to process his depression. As we looked to the roots of his current pain, he told us stories about religiously authoritarian parents who never nurtured. His mother worked hard and had a major breakdown when he was very young, and she never recovered. After affirming that this was such a hard way to grow up, we asked if in this whole experience there was even a glimpse—a sapphire glimmer—of love from his parents. None, he said at first, but when he asked Jesus to show him something, a story came to mind:

> I remember visiting mother when I was about 24. By then I was pretty anesthetized on anti-depressants, so I didn't relate. I left without saying goodbye to her. Days later, a letter came from her—rebuking me for not saying goodbye, but adding, "Don't you know I love you?"
>
> Up till now I've focused on her rebuke and my inability to relate. But in retelling this story, I get

a different view. I can see my mother did love me under all the illness, hard work, providing...under so much pain. I am beginning to discover I was loved, am loved. A part of me is getting unlocked. It's overwhelming. I've been really attracted to relational theology but now I have a story from my own life. A different way of seeing myself and others that has cut through my stifling inner darkness. I'm so grateful.

This glimmer, this hint of love in the pain of his parents' emotional absence, was a clue to his healing. When he did that digging with Jesus, Daniel did find a sapphire of love buried there—a true sign of the presence of Jesus.

Using the Sapphire Themes

The benefit of helping people connect their stories to one of the biblical sapphires is that it anchors this treasure to their name, their history, and the presence of Jesus as He intervenes. Then their story connects them to God's bigger story and can be revisited when they're seeking refreshment in the promise they received.

I, Dorothy, discovered a sapphire of assurance right in the darkest story of my life. After several years of blessed prayer healing ministry, all the excitement of seeing people healed began to dull my focus on Jesus as the only Healer. But all sense of my own importance in the healing process was abruptly halted with the death of my only brother.

He was a brilliant doctor and businessman who always outshone me in intelligence and vision. In his early years of studying medicine, he was an effective evangelist on the university campus. Later he despised our humble Christian upbringing with our emphasis on serving the poor and broken. His bitterness towards my parents' offering him only a Christian life option was distressing to me. My parents' health suffered, and my father stopped his beloved preaching and teaching as he took 1 Timothy 3:5 literally: how could he take care of God's church when his own son rejected the faith? I vacillated between secret criticism and deep love for my brother. I never fully resolved this tension, particularly as my parents grew weaker and their prayers for his return to the faith remained unanswered. Then one day after chairing a high-level corporate meeting, my brother committed suicide in one of his vineyards.

As I emerged from viewing his body, I was sickened by the horror that I had so judged my brother. How could I have poured out so much more unquestioning love to so many different people in ministry than I did to my own brother? At that moment a huge rainbow circled the funeral parlor. Immediately I knew God would never forsake His own—not my brother, not me, not any of us. This rainbow story contained a sapphire of assurance in the midst of unrelenting pain.

Not long after his death, we discovered that disturbing past events and hidden traumas had haunted his relationships. No wonder he abandoned the confines of our conservative faith. The dark currents in my seemingly good family story were demanding my embrace. My story was intertwined with my brother's story, not on two separate (committed versus uncommitted) tracks. I was his equal, a needy candidate for healing grace. The sapphire in my rainbow story still calls me to offer an accepting embrace of others' messy pain stories.

I recently met Adele, who knew nothing of these sapphire scriptures. She also doubted if the story she had told me, one that renewed her joy, was actually a story of the presence of Jesus. One day in her despair about her circumstances, she was just staring at the ground. Then she was startled to see sapphires inexplicably scattered through the dirt. Yes, beautiful blue sparkles. She was amazed and knew it was something encouraging from the Lord, but she wasn't sure what. Imagine our mutual delight when we shared that our stories of Jesus' presence are sapphires, glimmering His transforming hope into our pain and hopelessness.

Activities for Application

1. Read through each of the biblical sapphire stories. Which resonates with you the most?

2. Write or share with others about your own discovery of a sapphire in your pain story. If you don't have one, pray with someone else for Jesus to show you where your difficult story glimmers with His presence.

3. Guide someone through the process of discovering sapphires in their pain stories.

[33] Strong's *Hebrew Lexicon* #5601 and #5608.
[34] Other sapphire stories are found in Exodus 39:11, Ezekiel 28:13, and Revelation 21:19.
[35] We sometimes call this 'the sapphire test.'

PART FOUR:

EXPRESS THANKS TO HIM

10

CELEBRATE AND CONTINUE

IN THE FIRST THREE stages of the LIFE process, the person seeking healing has discovered something about the heart that Jesus gave them—how they were designed, what it's like to act like themselves, how to stay connected to Jesus and others. In this last stage, we companion them as they celebrate—as they live out of their true hearts.

It's so freeing when our passion, our purpose, and our pain all come together. It's such a relief to give the management of our hearts and our hurts to Jesus and to see the changes He is making in our stories. We are privileged to see definite signs of growth, of suffering well even if our circumstances don't change. We're humbled to find our God-given characteristics, even how our wounds can be used by Jesus to put us in touch with our true hearts, and to flourish as we resolve the lies we've lived by. The person's natural welling-up response to all of this can be embraced, affirmed, and encouraged as a regular part of their new life rhythm.

The Bible is full of celebrations and physical mementos of God's work, such as Miriam's spontaneous song
after the Egypt exit (Exodus 15), the annual Passover
celebration (Exodus 12), and monuments built to mark
a miraculous river crossing (Joshua 4:3-7). Affirmation
and celebration are important for making lasting change.
Celebration marks the end of the prayer session, but the
beginning of long-term healing connections. The ongoing
practice of the presence of Jesus continues to multiply
healing in our lives.

Celebrating Together

WHETHER THE PERSON has experienced the full LIFE process or only one or two steps, they have likely experienced
some healing that they want to celebrate by the end of the
session. A joyful energy for celebrating will flow from the
person who has now experienced healing, while the leader
and/or companion can support and enrich the expression.

As leaders, we bring the focus of the celebration to Jesus,
our Healer, and His call to make healing a way of life. Quieting prayer may celebrate something new Jesus has shown
the person. Then, to make the discovery more concrete,
we've guided people in countless types of celebration
activities at this stage: filling out certificates,[36] writing
thank-you notes, creating art books with each page pic-
turing a presence-of-Jesus encounter, writing songs and
poems, committing to healing habits, sharing the process
with friends, worshipping together—anything that feels
natural and helps to express their healing joy. These activities can wrap up the session or be assigned for later.

Before we part ways, the leader or companion reviews the session to explore further discoveries in the presence of Jesus. They re-tell what they have seen and ask questions. A final prayer thanks Jesus in detail for the work He has done. We offer blessings to the person who has experienced healing. Remembering that pain is often layered (see Chapter 8), so we may schedule another session with the person after celebrating what has been done so far. We assure the person that any unfinished stories will be held gently until we meet again.

Connecting to the Wider Story

THE SCRIPTURES ARE always calling us to see ourselves in His story. When we participate, it's like we become co-authors of the biblical story by filling out eternal themes with our own life details. The biblical writers say: don't tack God on to your story; allow yourself to be sought after and found inside His larger healing story.

Jo came to us with a deeply buried pain. Only after several sessions with us did she share that her grandfather regularly raped her in very young childhood. We held her hand as she went back into the room with Jesus, and she remembered: "While it happened, I focused on the hum of the air-conditioner. That hum became the gentle movement of angel's wings, assuring me that I could survive."

Later in my devotions, I read Ezekiel 10 and pondered his amazing visions of God's throne and the angels. Then came this image: "And the sound of the wings of the cherubim was heard as far as the outer court, like the voice of God Almighty when He speaks" (Ezekiel 10:5, RSV).

I thought immediately of Jo's story and her angel wings. At our next meeting, I shared this verse about Ezekiel's linking God's voice to the sounds of angels' wings. I asked her what God had said to her in the sound of the angel's wings. She's had years to ponder this: "The angel wings were so loud it blocked out his noise and allowed my mind to wander away from this terrible deed to focus on shiny colors which reflected only light. I believe these wings were God saying, 'I am protecting you.'"

Connecting to the Scripture helped Jo see that she is a part of God's wider story. She now offers this same angel-wing protection and comfort to many others in their time of distress, continuing her healing journey toward a much wider focus.

Celebrating by Obeying

OUR SESSIONS OFTEN end with brave commitments to live more storied, joyful lives with Jesus. Yes, this does require bravery—as author Brennan Manning tells us, "The most radical demand of the Christian faith lies in summoning the courage to say 'yes' to the present risenness of Jesus Christ."[37] Our "yes" commitment needs to be a daily, moment-by-moment response: "Lord Jesus, You are present now, right now in Your risen power, right now in the very life I have, not in the life I wished I had. It's a yes from me."

Even after having an arresting encounter with Jesus and refreshing His presence in our stories, keeping this 'yes' commitment can be incredibly difficult. Those old habits of trying to control, manage, and rationalize our pain are disturbingly automatic. The good news is that while we pursue healing, we never go back to where we started. We have experienced the heart Jesus gave us, and we know how to enter the presence of Jesus again—with encouragement and time to learn the practice of doing so. And it does take practice!

The writings of Brother Lawrence, the lowly seventeenth-century monk, inspire us to practice the presence of God. He battled huge challenges to say a constant 'yes' to the risen Jesus: cooking for 100 monks, complicated marketing for provisions, mending their sandals, coping with his many disabilities. But is his 'yes' possible for others, for us?

Below are a few insights from Brother Lawrence that have encouraged us, and those who have prayed with us, over the years.[38] We recommend sharing these quotes with those who want to celebrate Jesus by inviting Him into the daily rhythms of their lives.

Simple Attentiveness

"I gave up all devotions and prayers that were not required and I devote myself exclusively to remaining always in His holy presence. I keep myself in His presence by simple attentiveness and a general loving awareness of God that I call 'actual presence of God' or better, a quiet and secret conversation of the soul with God that is lasting."

Accepting God's Hospitality

"Far from chastening me, this King, full of goodness and mercy, lovingly embraces me, seats me at His table, waits on me Himself, gives me the keys to His treasures, and treats me in all things as His favorite. He converses with me and takes delight in me in countless ways...yet ever more caressed by God. This is what I see from time to time while in His holy presence."

Every Moment Holy

"The times of activity are not at all different from the hours of prayer...for I possess God as peacefully in the commotion of my kitchen, where often enough several people are asking me for different things at the same time, as I do when kneeling before the Blessed Sacrament."

Praying Simply

"To those who set out upon this practice let me suggest a few words, such as, 'My God, I am wholly Yours.' 'O, God of love, I love You with all my heart.' 'Lord, make my heart even as Your own' or such words as love prompts at the moment...Moreover, as I worked, I would continue to hold familiar conversations offering to Him my little acts of service and entreating the unfailing assistance of His grace."

Treasuring His Presence

"There is no way of life in the world more agreeable or delightful than continual conversation with God; only those who practice and experience it can understand this."

Frank Laubach (1884-1970), a long-term missionary in the Philippines, decided to test Brother Lawrence's practice of the presence of God. He wrote, "This year I have started out trying to live all my waking moments in a conscious listening to the inner voice, asking without ceasing, 'What, Father, do you desire said or done this minute?'"[39] He discovered that reshaping his busy life to this revolutionary practice of God's "here-ness" only increased his effectiveness in developing a worldwide literacy campaign to alleviate poverty and injustice. It allowed Laubach to fulfil his life goal: "I must see God in them and they must see God in me."[40]

Developing Healing Habits

RECENT SCIENCE TELLS us that our brains are plastic—moldable, changeable.[41] No one is doomed to live forever out of their pain-filled stories. We can develop new brain pathways that take us more directly to joy, quiet, and our stories of healing, instead of pain and anxious thoughts.

And yet the old habits are powerful, strangely comforting, and cemented in deep untruths about ourselves, others, and Jesus. This is why new habits—including joy building, quieting, and remembering our healing stories—take a long time to become part of us. The consensus is that they take at least six weeks of regular practice, one habit at a time. Neuroscientists call this developing a new neural pathway. We are happy when we're able to partner with people over these six weeks and beyond. We teach and keep in mind these three steps to developing new habits:

1. Recognize Cues to the Old Habit

Instead of getting mad at ourselves, doubting, or blaming the devil and others, we arrest the old habit by connecting to Jesus as we ask: What pain am I responding to here? How are my habits masking this pain?

2. Go Straight to Jesus

As quickly as possible, we interrupt this automatic process to this old habit. We pray something like this: "Here it is again, Lord Jesus. This is my way of disconnecting from You, my pain, myself. Now I'm coming straight to You." Develop the habit that most effectively arrests your negative pathway—quieting, joy building, etc. Stay in His presence until His peace absorbs the pain. Do this over and over until going to Jesus is our first response.

3. Celebrate

Express thanks for the new habit by practicing it daily. Keeping a journal of your progress helps you to celebrate your new neural healing pathway or habit.

This is a pattern that all of us need to learn to practice for ourselves. We can daily include activities[42] that challenge us to build joy, quiet, and remember our stories between sessions. At the beginning of each prayer session, we check for progress in developing habits and connections with Jesus, others, and ourselves.

In our trusting peer relationship, developing new habits is a tender collaborative process. We ask, "How can we strengthen your commitment to new healing habits? What works best for you?" We offer encouragement to any sign of moving toward the new commitment. Our battles are always fiercer than we care to admit. We need one another for healing, as Laubach says, "There is no defeat until one loses God, and then all is defeat."[43] Joy groups that help us live in the always-present nearness of Jesus are the focus of our next chapter.

Activities for Application

1. At this point, we have covered every phase of the LIFE process for individual sessions. Pause and review the four stages. What aspects will you integrate into your conversations and into your regular prayer times with others?

2. Choose a healing habit (joy, quiet, or remembering) to focus on for the next six weeks. Review the activities in the relevant chapter, as well as those listed in Appendix B. Keep a journal, noting what works well and what you might recommend to others.

3. Practice the presence of Jesus each day for a week. Identify His presence in ordinary events. Celebrate His creative incarnations communally as well as personally.

[35] Available online at *ServantPartnersPress.org/SeedsOfJoy*.

[37] Brennan Manning, *Abba's Child: The Cry of the Heart for Intimate Belonging* (Colorado Springs: NavPress, 1994), 80.

[38] Brother Lawrence and Frank Laubach, *Practicing His Presence*, ed. G. Edwards (Jacksonville: Seedsowers, 1973), as quoted in Michael Frost, *Exiles: Living Missionally in a Post-Christian Culture* (Erina, NSW: Strand, 2006), 65-69.

[39] Brother Lawrence and Laubach, *Practicing His Presence*, 22.

[40] Ibid., 22.

[41] Norman Doidge, The Brain That Changes Itself (London: Penguin, 2007).

[42] See Appendix B.

[43] Brother Lawrence and Laubach, *Practicing His Presence*, 22.

11

JOY GROUPS

HEALING IS ALWAYS RELATIONAL. As one pastor once turned the phrase, "It takes village to raise a child, and it takes a whole church to heal its members." Sadly, even in churches and mission groups, many remain isolated and unable to connect. Alone is not good, says God in Genesis 2:18. We aren't designed to do life alone, and we can't find healing and joy that way.

Neuroscientists tell us that synchronizing, or developing minds with a capacity to regularly connect empathetically with others, is essential for good brain health. Being alone is damaging for mental health. Groups can normalize pain so its power is reduced. Finding commonality contributes to emotional rest as well as a healthy sense of smallness—that our individual problems, though pressing, are a drop in the ocean of human experience, both good and bad.

Joy groups sprang from our prayer ministry, but we cannot take credit for developing them. It was a group of friends, after beginning healing journeys in our sessions and seminars, who realized something was missing from our model. As one member recounts, "It only took one person to say, 'We need to go on and do this regularly as a group together.' We started meeting every Monday night to share joy stories, and we haven't stopped for seven years. We used to belong to Dorothy and George, but now we belong to one another." This story has deeply encouraged us.

Finding Joy People

JOY GROUPS CAN take place in any context. They can be a sort of alternative home group in a church-based context. They can convene in retirement homes, college campuses, long-term hospitals, prisons, apartment building court-yards, or community centers. We are glad to hear about all of the places where people are gathering to share joy.

As this list indicates, joy groups work well for every generation of adults—the unique lonelinesses of our twenties and thirties, middle age, and older adulthood all cry out for connection. As mentioned in the Introduction, we rarely work with children under the age of sixteen because their neurological development is still in process. Our approach is to resource their parents, who are then equipped to model LIFE to their children.

Some groups welcome people with mental illness. They are not therapy groups, but with gentle quieting together and the telling of joy stories, more healing can be released. One leader who has been diagnosed with Bipolar 2 disorder comments, "When I met Dorothy and George, I was desperately broken and had given up hope of ever being healed and of God speaking to me. I still experience brokenness, but I know without a doubt that God loves me to the core. I know I can come to Him in any state and connect to Jesus. It's like a breath of fresh air from God. This is what prayer healing has done for me. I feel love in many areas of pain." She encourages others like herself to stay on their medications, and to take the group as an opportunity to grow closer to others and to Jesus. She says for herself and others like her that the group "adds structure to our chaos" and allows Jesus to break through stigmas and negative self-views. The leader shared, "Gradually we we hear less and less of those old statements—'I'm a failure,' or, 'Why would Jesus or others accept someone like me?' This is everything to us. Our role is not to provide clinical therapy to the mentally ill, but to companion them in connecting to Jesus, others, and themselves in joy and in truth."

If this book has sparked a concept for your joy group, start inviting potential members to tell their stories of the presence of Jesus in their lives—joy stories. Share what you've learned about how the brain processes joy and pain, and ask them if they would like to build joy in the presence of Jesus with others. Don't let yourself think you need advanced theological qualifications. The practice of the presence of Jesus alone helps us reach out and draw others into His peace and joy. Start with a small group and allow it to grow over time.

Leading In Joy

Joy Groups are communities of leaders—self-run teams, not guided by a curriculum or a single prayer leader. As one group member said, "It's really Jesus who leads it.

Taking turns in guiding sessions, facilitating the sharing, and choosing different activities keeps us fresh. The group gives us resources for our personal lives as well, so leading is more energizing than exhausting." Often, committed group members will meet before sessions to prepare and pray together.

The next sections explore how current joy groups are using the LIFE process in a group setting. The steps of LIFE are the same as those we've been examining, though usually they're modified for a group setting. For joy groups, the LIFE process is not a checklist! Our longest-running group has told us, "We've been doing the same two things for the past seven years: quieting and sharing joy stories. And it's still fresh." Feel free to use the LIFE process in a way that works for you.

L – Live in the Presence of Jesus

WORSHIP TOGETHER

Singing, prayers of praise, anointing with oil, or taking communion might help a group enter tangibly into the presence of Jesus. This expression may depend on the denomination and/or level of religious experience of members, and should feel like a natural expression for the group's sense of community. For some members, the group is their only church—their safe place.

JOY BUILDING

Members love to start with a joy story from the previous week. They might share joy objects (or tell jokes, or play a song) as a kind of show-and-tell. Leaders might bring or create a visual to reflect upon together, or provide colorful scarves to represent being enveloped in the joy of Jesus. More joy building activities are listed in Appendix B.

QUIETING PRAYER

Often leaders will direct the quieting in new groups, asking for someone (or each person in turn) to volunteer a quality of Jesus they are thankful for. Quieting also emerges out of gratitude questions that focus on the group, such as, "What are we discovering together about Jesus that we could not discover about ourselves?" or "What aspect of Jesus have you grown to appreciate by being together?" Some real answers have included the following: "We're accepted." "Life is noisy, but we find peace here." "No one gets excluded for their mental illness or depression." "We belong to one another and to Jesus." "We've discovered the presence of the Holy Spirit in every person." Any or all of these responses can be repeated back in quieting prayer to Jesus.

Although it may seem odd, group members have reported that quieting is actually easier in the context of a trusted group. The collective breathing and calm provide a rhythm for our anxious brains and cradles us in connection. As in one-on-one sessions, groups will return to Jesus in quieting prayer with each new discovery about Him, and at points of tension or pain.

I – Identify Past Stories of His Presence

STORIES OF THE WEEK

If not already used as an opener, group members may here take turns telling stories from their week. Each member shares what is comfortable, and others listen—only with questions (e. g., How did you feel in that story? Where did you sense Jesus with you in that time?) that help connect to their true hearts behind the stories. Any response should be gentle, non-invasive, and should not include advice for the person's situation.

HERITAGE STORIES

Leaders may prompt past-history stories about members' early lives, people who have influenced them for good, times they've sensed the presence of Jesus, etc. At some point, we encourage groups to allow space for each member to share their whole story. Any of these can be recorded in audio form or from a note taker into a group joy journal, with the storyteller's permission.

RETELLING STORIES

There is a lot of joy in repeating a member's story back to them as a whole group, each person adding distinctive insights. Members can share what they've valued about the person and Jesus in the story. In telling their stories together, group members feel understood, validated, and accepted, and they readily turn story insights into prayers of blessing.

RESPONSE ACTIVITY

The rotating leader will create or choose an activity (some options are listed in Appendix B) to help people explore and connect to their stories. Activities can involve writing, drawing, acting, or any other form of embodiment. In time, the group may settle on some favorites for regular use.

F – Find Him in Those Moments When He Seemed Absent

PAIN STORIES

Sufficient resources of joy and quiet create comfort for the sharing of pain stories. Whether it was a bad week or a recurring negative memory, members gently companion the person in inviting Jesus to come again into the situation. The person will generally benefit from sitting in silence during this process, but members may sometimes ask questions to help a person find seeds of healing or sapphires of Jesus' joy and presence in their past stories (see Chapters 6 and 9), or simply say, "What aspect of Jesus is encouraging or strengthening you to face this problem?" It is important that members not judge, interpret, or give advice to each other's situations, but refer all to Jesus in conversational prayer.

FOLLOWING UP

A person with more joy resources may make themselves available for visiting later in the week if a challenging pain emerges. This companioning in a person's pain draws on the LIFE resources in the previous chapters. Retreats together to a pleasant place may also give members space to process their pain.

MORE QUIETING

Difficult meetings can benefit from pausing to quiet (every five or ten minutes, perhaps). Invite any person to initiate quieting through some discreet hand signal or cue. You may also pass a small re-focusing object, such as a cross, around the circle as people share, reminding them to quiet within themselves and in the group.

E – Express Thanks to Him

CELEBRATION

We commemorate what Jesus has done by filling out certificates,[44] creative worship, and eating together. We celebrate our progress in tangible ways.

CLOSING PRAYER

Likewise, the leader's prayer covers all that is discovered in the group. How are we journeying towards one another and Jesus? What changes can we celebrate (try filling in "we used to … but now…")? Who is our special joy person of the week? How can we spread joy to others? Let's thank Jesus together.

Joy Groups for Deep Connections

Joy groups truly connect members to Jesus, others, and themselves, sometimes in unexpected ways. In one group, a member had an unexpected stroke that left her paralyzed. The group now has one meeting each month in her palliative care facility. One member tells us, "We can still quiet together and retell her joy stories. She can't speak, but we point to her photos and her expressions of joy or sadness to tell us how to pray. We discovered that she can still participate in singing, even in our anointing. Once I put the oil on her finger and she wiped it from ear to ear and down my nose! We both cried for joy. Despite her disability, she can build joy; she remains firm in connections to us, her own story, and Jesus. For all of us, the presence of Jesus in these meetings is palpable—more powerful than strokes."

We've also been surprised by the way that joy connections radiate out beyond the bounds of the group. Our practice of joyful remembrance has become communal. At one community mental health center, this happens in a very tangible way. Our leaders work with people in various stages of dementia to record their stories. Photos are added to make beautiful memory books. After one woman was taken into care, her husband dropped in and was given a copy of her story. He asked who wrote it, not imagining it could be his precious wife. He had no idea she could remember the stories. Sheer joy for the preserved connection and revived tenderness shone through his tears. Healing in one person creates healing connections in all of their relationships.

Activities for Application

1. What has been your best group experience? Write, draw, or share about a time when a group has contributed to your healing.

2. Which group example or idea is most intriguing to you? What might you want to integrate into a joy group?

3. If you plan to create a joy group, write out a to-do list and begin talking to others.

---

[44] Those we use are available online at *ServantPartnersPress.org/SeedsOfJoy*.

12

ONWARD INTO HEALING

WHAT IF WE ALL lived out of our stories of the presence of Jesus? What if we cultivated the healing seeds in our stories, and lived in the truth we found in them? What future awaits us on the other side of our traumas?

Healing means so much more than the removal of pain. We don't seek healing in our own lives and in the lives of others just to return to our old ideas of normalcy—something neutral, un-exciting. We tell stories in the presence of Jesus to learn who we are, to live in the power of His Gospel in our daily lives, to find our small part in God's wider story. We become storytellers and story-listeners to connect with others, to offer them a personal connection with Jesus in their own lived experiences, to unlock Jesus' path to healing in them rather than our own ideas about solutions. Though unresolved pain can drive us to seek healing, it is only a symptom of deeper disconnects. Once restored, we find more capacity for joyful relational connection with God, others, and ourselves in our lives than we could possibly imagine.

Signposts of the Healing Journey

SO FAR, WE HAVE traced the steps of a LIFE prayer session and reviewed ways to adapt those steps for joy groups. Yet we recognize that our ultimate aim is not just good sessions, but the unleashing of Jesus' healing in people's whole lives. In many cases, we don't get to see this. In one-off meetings or spontaneous encounters, we trust that Jesus sparked something in our time together, and that He will invite them into a continued journey toward healing and joy.

Other times, we have an opportunity to develop a relationship with someone over time, whether through regular sessions or through a new friendship. We don't share the average professional's constraint around befriending those we meet with, as they are not our clients. In cases like this, when we have an opportunity to develop a healing relationship with someone, it's important to think about what we're looking for as we move forward together over the long arc of healing. Similarly, what do we look for in our own lives, as we track our own healing journeys over the decades?

When we live out of our stories of the presence of Jesus, we connect more consistently to Him. We can draw on His healing resources to:

- Process our pain more fully
- Go on to maturity
- Accept the slow, unfinished bits
- Live more fully from our true centers—from the hearts Jesus gave us

Processing Our Pain More Fully

Living out of our stories of the presence of Jesus does not mean a pain-free life. It does mean a commitment to progress along the pain processing pathway so that we can reconnect to Jesus in our old and new pains. It's right there in His presence that we discover the seeds of healing: being nurtured by joy, quieting, relating, growing, and living out of our true hearts.[45] It allows us to see how even our suffering is not wasted but fits into God's bigger story.

Shelley's journey holds a remarkable story of processing her pain in a way that is transforming her life. She told us:

> I was doing well in my life in England—at the top of my profession, with a successful husband and three children, and no debt. My great desire to live in the warmer climate of Australia was not daunted by 10 years of immigration obstacles. But in our new warmer life, our professional qualifications were not recognized, unscrupulous people ripped off our business, and our marriage failed. I was stripped down to nothing.
>
> Right inside this turmoil a new calling clarified: to be an immigration agent. I use my negotiating skills and I pray for miracles to see the most impossible visas granted. A Burmese Muslim asylum seeker begged me to work and pray for his wife to be released from immigration detention, and after 18 months (instead of five years), she was free. The favor of God, we both agreed,

defied the tense immigration controversies. Life for me and my clients is still uncertain, but in my nothingness, I have everything, because I have Jesus and the unfolding of His promise, given to me four years ago, that He would heal me and use me to heal others. My greatest need has become an open doorway to multiple multi-national healing opportunities.

How could Shelley go on in peace in a new land that has brought so much nothingness? A childhood encounter with Jesus, confirmed in several later stories, affirmed for Shelley that she was not meant to live a fruitless winter life. This was much more than a call to a different climate; it was a heart discovery of finding warmth and fullness in her bleak nothingness. Many tumbles, many shut doors, still many unsolvable dilemmas, and long grieving—but she's not blocked in pain. The coordinating theme of her stories is: "No one, nothing, can take Jesus away from me."

Through the LIFE process, we hope to companion many others as they discover how Jesus' presence can bring joy resources for new healing into their pain processing pathways, just as Shelley did.

Going On to Maturity

Becoming mature, growing into Christ, is the biggest challenge of the Christian community (Colossians 1:28). Even when we want to grow, we run up against so many blockages to maturity that indicate our relationships are more fear-based than love-based. How different it would be if we had the courage, the support, and the skills to mature!

Dr. Jim Wilder classifies five stages of maturity which may or may not correspond with age, identifying the primary challenge of each[46]:

Stage	Primary Challenge	Primary Resulting Problem
Infant	Learning and receiving with joy	Weak or stormy relationships, can't trust or regulate own emotions
Child	Taking care of oneself	Not taking responsibility for oneself, living in fantasy or addiction
Adult	Taking care of one other person	Lacks capacity for satisfying relationships, self-centered, controlling
Parent	Sacrificially taking care of others	Distant/conflicting family relationships, can't accept support when needed
Elder	Sacrificially taking care of the community	Withdrawal into self, community health declines

As Wilder points out, we may be stuck at an infant stage if we have never been helped to develop trust others or regulate our emotions, for example. Resources to master the maturity challenges at each level are found in the presence of Jesus and in a healing community.

Maturing is a challenging, patience-demanding process, not a spiritual gift. The questions get bigger, the severity of our deceptions more overwhelming, and our trust appears more like self-preservation. Yet in focusing a healing process around the presence of Jesus in our stories, we begin to understand that His way is growth, not just symptom relief.

As we move along in maturity, we move beyond blame and demanding approval from those who are incapable of giving this. Our foundational needs can be met with Jesus and with His community. Lebu had tried every way possible to earn his mother's love—provide financially, relieve her pressures, rescue her, cover for her—with little response. The hurt from this lost relationship went deep back into childhood abandonment. He told us,

> I've never been able to understand why my mother abandoned me. She left me in the village for years, with relatives who used me. They forced me to sell vegetables rather than go to school. One day my vegetable cart was stolen, but they wouldn't believe me and sent me to sleep in the filthy dog cage in the freezing cold. I don't know how I survived. For years I have been in that dog cage—from all the bitterness, the aching for my mother's acceptance and approval, and the constant abuse from apartheid and my own pain.
>
> After we prayed together, I looked at the stars in the night sky. I sensed Jesus saying, "You can be free of all that pain." I can forgive and be forgiven; I can be released from waiting for my mother's lost love. After all of these years, I'm out of that cage with greater freedom to serve my people in their pain.

As for Lebu, the healing seeds of our presence of Jesus stories are the resources for our growing in maturity—becoming more like Him. As George says, "That's real joy—my greatest joy in this work."

Accepting the Slow, Unfinished Bits

As we live out of our stories of the presence of Jesus, we begin to discover that most of our answered prayers, our quests for meaning, come out of the larger story He is composing for us. It is hard to come to terms with the fact that this larger story will also include pain, slowness, and promising pieces that just trail off. Those delays and dark nights expose our fears, but also refine our desires to continue. In the mystery of pain, we realize that Jesus is growing us more into Himself and that the best place to see His connections in our story is in the disappointments, the losses, and the unfinished bits.

A group of missionaries among the urban poor in Los Angeles were compelled to respond to city authorities' plan build a giant regional waste facility near schools, homes, and playing fields in their already disadvantaged neighborhood. The group took steps to unite churches with community organizations against this injustice. Never before had the city's use of power been challenged by such a large and diverse group of residents. This was not a quick, easy journey, as the moneyed opposition fiercely and publicly maligned and belittled the humble protesters.

The missionaries' initiative set their attempt at justice-making in the framework of God's plans to redeem our whole cosmos, including our individual lives. Members were gradually open to pray for the opposition and even for their own problems and sicknesses. Communal, sinful injustice was confessed and challenged as the old secular-sacred divides dissolved. Christian workers were drawn beyond personally attacking the perpetrators of injustice to trying to be more like Jesus: standing with the poor, working for justice, and even finding ways to build bridges of communication with their maligners.

Amazingly in the process they discovered the parallel reality of seeking communal and personal healing. As one missionary said, "I'm discovering more healing for my own past experience of abuse by standing with others against communal injustice. And we even have fun and experience joy! We women who have been working for environmental justice have bought dollar store tiaras and now call ourselves 'the Queens of Trash.'"

The coalition ultimately couldn't stop the building of the facility, but they did make significant gains for environmental health in their community in the form of better regulation. Most importantly, they gained a deep knowledge of the destructive sources of injustice in their city as well as forming new and healing community relationships. Justice-making is unfinished, but many are still companions together on their communal and personal healing journeys.

Healing always takes place in the context of our world's messiness. Our hope is that people would feel peace in the chaos, in the unfinished bits, and in the stubborn internal pains that linger. We understand all of it—*all* of it—to be under the guidance of God, our Sovereign Storyteller.

Living from Our True Hearts

Our presence of Jesus stories resource us to live out of His view of ourselves. Under all the layers of pain, regret, and disappointments, we discover in our stories that the hearts that God gave us are still there. We can find personally crafted answers to questions like, "What are the values of my heart? Who recognizes my value? How are these expressed in my life calling? In my ordinary life events?" Understanding and living out of our true identities in Jesus is ultimately the only source of satisfaction we can have.

Ash and Kim believed they had a calling to cross-cultural mission, so they intentionally chose to teach in an indigenous community in rural Australia. However, depression, anxiety, and marriage difficulties made them feel as if they were unqualified for mission. Thankfully for many, their story continues:

> In the midst of all of this, the local pastor came to us, saying, "Guys, we need you to run the local youth group that consists of 30 young Aboriginal males and 20 white girls. We won't accept no for an answer, as you guys are the only choice!" Well, from night one, the young people's belief in us as a couple gave us a glimpse of what our relationship with Christ and each other could really be.
>
> We soon got a frantic call from Ronnie, a student in the group: "Something terrible has happened. A truck crushed my pop's car. Everyone was in it, now there's just me and my sister."

We came quickly, and just held them and cried out to Jesus. The next few weeks was spent around different kitchen tables hearing stories of family, stories of Jesus and being together. The presence of Jesus was so strong and sustaining. We finally accepted that there is no qualification for mission apart from the presence of Jesus in, through, and around us.

For Kim and Ash, following their call aligned them with the heart Jesus gave them, allowing them to fully express and live out of their best selves. This isn't a personal accomplishment, but the presence of Jesus filling them, flowing mysteriously to others. They have since made significant contributions to that community and to many other communities in Asia as well, by teaching English through parables. Their ministry continues to draw tuk-tuk drivers, Muslim educators, refugees, and university students to discover God's purposes through His stories and theirs.

We hope that we and every person we pray with would have the courage to step into a life lived out of our true hearts, the hearts Jesus gave us for others.

Healing People Healing People

THE PHRASE "hurt people hurt people" shines a light on the way that pain moves through families and communities, but it is not the whole story. People on healing journeys also pull one another forward, toward Jesus and their new lives. As a community we aim to be "healing people healing people"—not *healed* people, with our own internal work tidily complete, but people developing this new life together. This has two heavy implications for us as we finish this book and go off to practice Jesus' presence through story.

First, we must remember that our journey of healing is not separate from those who come to us in deep pain. We may be a prayer leader today, and a person seeking healing tomorrow. It takes constant checks of humility to remember this, to seek the maintenance of our own pain processing pathways, and to live out of our own stories. Our healing is our best gift to others, and we cannot neglect it.

The other insight, perhaps the most important in this book, is that we are helping others to become powerful companions of others' healing. The people seeking prayer healing today are also tomorrow's prayer leaders and companions. Our greatest hope is to make ourselves redundant as people and communities live in the presence of Jesus and find resources for their own healing. The work belongs to Jesus, and the best we can do for others is to get out of His way.

The biggest compliment we have ever heard about our prayer sessions was, "In my encounter with Jesus, He met me. You weren't there." May it always be so.

Activities for Application

1. Reflecting on the signposts for the healing journey, where are you in your own long-term healing process? Share how you or someone close to you has grown.

2. Reflect on what you've read about the LIFE process, the human brain, and Jesus' heart to heal. What will you take with you? Write, draw, or share with others what you will take away.

3. Create a plan to integrate your takeaways into your life and ministry. What are your goals for praying with others?

[45] See Chapter 6.

[46] This table is distilled from his Maturity Indicators. Jim Wilder, *Living for the Heart Jesus Gave You* (Pasadena: Shepherd's House, 2004), 51-55.

ACKNOWLEDGEMENTS

My greatest source of joy in this book journey has been the many deepening relationships. My first thanks is to my precious husband George, whose joy-filled, faith sustaining companionship has directed me in love and prayer. Our grace-transformed unity is the priceless gift of healing in our marriage and softens our scarred efforts to serve over the years. Be aware that though I am the author here, George is the reason that people call this ministry "so gentle, so Jesus focused." Then our good friend Jeff has patiently transformed my scrappy notes into a readable document, despite health challenges and technical glitches. His joy in serving us has spurred us on. Elizabeth Rhea, my editor, has believed in this project even through the challenges of my too-copious diversions. Without her and Bree Hsieh at Servant Partners Press, this focused process would not have been available for many to become healing companions. Servant Partners Co-General Directors Lisa and Derek Engdahl have offered us wider horizons for ministry in many countries where we have proved again and again that story-healing truly helps all peoples become more whole, become named. Helping hundreds of people reconnect to the One who names each person precious, names them Mine, is our greatest joy. This book distills a little of our continuing joy-filled journey.

APPENDICES:

APPENDIX A: LIFE PRAYER PROCESS OUTLINE AND PRAYER PROMPTS

APPENDIX B: INDEX OF EXERCISES

APPENDIX C: THE PAIN PROCESSING PATHWAY

APPENDIX A: LIFE PRAYER PROCESS OUTLINE AND PRAYER PROMPTS

These overviews summarize the CompanionLIFE prayer process. They can be used as scripts, or you can adapt them with your own language.

Individual Prayer

Live in the Presence of Jesus

Lord Jesus, come close to me right now. Help me focus on what I appreciate about You (choose a characteristic of Jesus to praise Him for, such as: *Jesus, You are my peace*). I quiet myself in Your presence by slowly breathing in and out while I pray this truth silently or out loud. (*Thank You, Jesus. You are my peace.*)

Identify Past Stories of His Presence

Please remind me of a story when I experienced You in this way (recall specific details: time, place, emotions, people, etc., when you knew Jesus as your peace or other characteristic you've named). Show me what I was like when I was in Your presence. How did You treat me? Help me to recognize the seeds of healing that You have placed in my story and how these seeds of joy affect my current situation or other past stories. I will continue to enjoy Your presence within my story.

Find Him In Those Moments When He Seemed Absent

Now, Lord, stay with me as I go to a difficult time or issue that is troubling me. Please come again in gentle power as You did in my quieting and story. I will move toward my pain while still connecting to You, and I will ask You to show me how You are with me here and now, and how You are with me in my current pain, and where You were in my past pain. I will stay in this painful place or memory until You flood it with Your peace. If I encounter some obstacle, I will ask: Jesus, what is blocking a renewed sense of Your peace? Stay with me while You show me Your truth and restore Your peace in this dark place.

Express Thanks to Him

Thank You for restoring Your peace. Keep me connected to You all the time. I want to live in Your presence. Help me to see the themes of Your presence in my stories. Chart my future by Your peace. Thank You for the way You have prepared me for any healing in my story of Your presence. I expand the scope of my story by linking it to a biblical story with a similar theme.

Companion Sessions

Live in the Presence of Jesus

Welcome to CompanionLIFE prayer healing. We are honored to be your companion as you connect to Jesus, your Healer. The aim of prayer healing is to resource you to live in the presence of Jesus, the optimum place for your ongoing healing. He wants to meet you personally and to restore His presence in all situations of your life.

Tell us briefly why you have come for prayer healing (just the core issues here).

Let's invite His presence with an opening prayer and anointing with oil.

(The companion is invited to participate in these.)

Let's build some joy before we proceed. (To the companion): Tell us what you value in your friend.

(If no companion): Tell us what you really enjoy. Who is with you as you face this problem? (Introduce and lead a joy-building activity from Appendix B.)

Let's now quiet together in the presence of Jesus. What do you appreciate about Jesus right now? As we do this, tell us any impressions or difficulties you have. (We do not proceed until the person is peaceful.)

Identify Past Stories of His Presence

Let's ask Jesus to remind you of a story when you sensed His presence (maybe in the same way you chose for quieting, e.g., He is my hope). Tell that story in detail—give it a name, place, date. What were you like in that story? How did Jesus treat you? What healing seeds did He place in your story?

Let's retell your story (ask companion to do this). Let's pray through it again to celebrate that you have experienced the presence of Jesus and know how He will treat you again.

Quiet again on any new insights from this retelling.

Find Him In Those Moments When He Seemed Absent

Are you ready/willing now to ask Jesus to come into that painful situation you mentioned before? Let's review how He will treat you (go over 'Identify' discoveries again).

Come, Lord Jesus—right inside this painful place. We wait together in Your presence until You restore Your peace. What would You like to say or do in this place?

Express Thanks to Him

We celebrate here how you have connected to Jesus right inside your pain. We revisit that painful place to check if it needs more immersion in the presence of Jesus.

Let's link your story to any biblical stories that celebrate a similar connection to Jesus. Then we discuss ways you can continue to practice healing habits for ongoing healing. CompanionLIFE certificates and other mementos can help you remember your prayer healing session.

Joy Groups

L – Live in the Presence of Jesus

Welcome to joy group! Our aim here is to share and build joy together in the presence of Jesus.

Let's worship together. (Planned or spontaneous: sing, dance, make art, etc.)

For this week's joy activity, let's... (See Appendix B)

What do you appreciate about Jesus tonight? OR What have you learned about Jesus by being here together? (Or similar.) Let's thank Jesus in quieting prayer: "Thank you, Jesus. You are our..."

I – Identify Past Stories of His Presence

When did you experience joy this week? OR Share about a joyful time in your life.

This week we're going to hear _____'s story. (We recommend that each member get a chance to tell a fuller version of their life story. This will take a larger portion of the session and can be done as a special series.)

What I heard in/valued about your story was... (each person should hear their story told back to them in this simple way at least once!)

This week, to respond to and remember our stories, let's... (See Appendix B)

F – Find Him In Those Moments When He Seemed Absent

(If pain stories emerge and nonverbal empathy is not sufficient.) What aspect of Jesus is encouraging or strengthening you to face this problem?

Let's return to Jesus in quieting prayer.

(Afterward, a leader might arrange one-on-one prayer time with the one who expressed pain.)

E – Express Thanks to Him

Let's commemorate what Jesus has done by... (Create a memento or remembrance of gratitude for what Jesus has done.)

Who would like to close in prayer, thanking Jesus for what we have discovered here together?

APPENDIX B: INDEX OF EXERCISES

Healing is connecting to Jesus, others, and ourselves. While some connecting is a gift that comes without our initiative or effort, other connecting needs to be practiced.

These exercises include bonding activities, story prompts, and response ideas to use throughout the LIFE prayer healing process. All activities focus on stories as they link us to God's wider healing. We use certificates to mark various firsts and challenges; these can be downloaded at *ServantPartnersPress.org/SeedsOfJoy*.

Live In the Presence of Jesus

These exercises celebrate the practice of the presence of Jesus as the optimum context for healing. Joy building and quieting are the two essential resources for helping you develop healing foundations.

Joy Building

MY JOY JOURNAL

List a joy moment from each day of the week. Record the time of day when you most need to replenish joy. Note the cumulative effect of joy building and share this with others who are doing this exercise. If repeated for several weeks, joy building will become a healing habit.

JOY PEOPLE

List three people (alive or dead) who appreciate you, bring you joy. Note their heart characteristics that help your joy and find ways to thank them. Also, model their kind of joy with others.

JOY WITH JESUS

Record for a week the ways you are receiving joy and building joy daily with Jesus (e. g., through a scripture, song, answered prayer, courage in despair, etc.). Turn these into appreciation prayers: "Thank You, Jesus. You are my..." Record how joy with Jesus affects your daily life. Creating joy certificates together multiplies joy.

JOY AND REST

Connect with your companion to share non-verbally your appreciation. Take two to three minutes. Don't stare. Take frequent rests. Then share the benefit of this joy/rest connection.

JOY TOGETHER STORIES

Tell a joy story of an experience together. What made it so good to be together? How did your companion bring you joy? Thank Jesus for what you discover in each other.

Photos, drawing, acting, and singing together increase the joy together.

JOY CREATING

Create, view, or listen to some form of music or art (e. g., collages, mosaics) together. Play some music, a story, act it out; play a game, take photos of nature—note how joy multiplies through creativity.

JOY JAR

As a family or group, make short notes about joy experiences and place these in a jar. Select notes at random to retell; act or sing these joy stories. It's good to relate these stories non-verbally too. Comment on how members build the family joy and their hearts behind these actions (e.g., sensitive, caring, etc.). Give prizes for the favorite, best retold story. Pray for one another as you build joy together even in difficult times.

JOY QUESTIONS

In shared meals, spend 10 minutes sharing events of the day. Ask questions like these: When did you feel you belonged? Who valued you today? Whom did you value? How did you act at your best today? How did you sense peace from Jesus today? (You will recognize these questions from Lehman's pain processing pathway. These questions are more specific for healing than "How was your day?") Focus on eye contact, expressing your feelings, and validating the feelings of others. How does this help you stay connected to one another and to Jesus?

NON-VERBAL STORIES

Using only your voice tones or facial expressions, tell a story of your day. Others guess what happened (include difficult, frustrating, overwhelming events). Someone else tells the story back non-verbally. Check for accuracy. How does this help you stay connected? Repeat this exercise with your favorite Bible stories. Guess what story is being told. How does this build your joy together?

JOY OF MEETING JESUS

Together discuss where you would have most liked to meet Jesus. Set some scenes. Act them out. Discuss what you would like to ask or share with Jesus at this scene—e.g., His birth (Luke 2: 8-15), His healing (Luke 8: 40-48), His celebrating (John 2: 1-11).

CATCH JOY

Form groups of 6 people. All must have glum faces. No smiling. One person is chosen to smile and then fling that smile to another person, who catches it and smiles. All others remain glum. If anyone smiles out of turn, you're out. The aim of this game is to prove that you can catch and pass on joy from one another and that in a joy-filled atmosphere it is very hard not to be joyful.

JOY SINGING

For large groups, form 2 groups of 6 people. Choose a song that all people know well. One group sings the song in harmony (after a little practice), or sings at different pitches or with different actions. The other group sings the song on the same note. Even if this is a mess, people realize that joy together grows more with diversity than with sameness.

JOY TOGETHER

Give groups of 5-6 people 3 soft balls. Synchronize by throwing the balls to one another as you count evenly to 10. If you get to 10 without dropping balls, you win. This simple game shows that there is joy in synchronizing together.

JOY BUCKET

The amount of joy we have indicates the degree to which we are confident and secure with God, others, and ourselves. In your life story, how full was/is your joy bucket? When were there joy deficits? Who were the people who filled your joy bucket? How did they do this? How do you pour out joy? Draw this out to chart your growth in joy and need of healing for joy deficits. Share with others. Encourage prayer healing for joy deficits.

SHARE JOY

Every day for the next week, aim to share joy with at least one person, giving clear signals that you are present with the person. This can be simple, like smiling, asking about their day, giving a small gift (plastic pearls, thank-you cards), going on an outing, sharing a book or music, worshipping together, or sharing a joke. Notice how their joy builds and yours too. Thank God that you can share joy.

JOY AUTOGRAPHS

At a group, pin a piece of paper onto the backs of each person. All write an appreciation of every person on this. Read these out for all to appreciate.

MOVE TOGETHER

Practice a simple dance step or funny walk together. What is satisfying/unsatisfying about this for helping you share joy?

JOY IN CREATION

Start with admiring beautiful nature pictures. Then read Psalm 8 as you each choose the picture that best relates to the psalm. Then reflect on the image of God (Genesis 1:26) in nature, in you. What makes it difficult to see the image of God in you, in others? How would things change if you made a habit of seeing the image of God both in nature and in ourselves?

What can you see about the image of God (the way God created them) even in difficult people? Give examples of doing this and turn these responses into prayers for people, e.g., "Thank you, Jesus, for this person's heart for justice. Even behind his rough outbursts I can see the way You made him to care for the needy. Thank You for what I can now see of Your image in him." Then commit to practicing this and to sharing the responses at the next group.

Quieting

RECORDING YOUR QUIETING PHRASES

Write down your chosen appreciation of Jesus as the focus of your quieting in the prayer healing session and in daily life. Keep a quieting journal to note your insights, life responses to regular quieting, and your developing ability to live in the presence of Jesus.

QUIET TOGETHER

Group quieting is connecting, bonding to one another and to Jesus. It celebrates both who you are and who you are becoming as you live together in the presence of Jesus. Group quieting is encouraged at pleasant and difficult moments in meetings so that decisions can be made in the presence of Jesus.

EXTENDED QUIETING

Quieting with Jesus long enough for His presence to grow bigger than the pain is the route to healing. You do this best by going over in detail the places, stories, music, scriptures, people, etc., where you have sensed His presence, and by staying there until you connect in peace to Him again. Often He reveals new healing insights as you extend your quieting.

SIMPLE QUIETING

Sit in a quiet place with a companion. Avoid talking or making eye contact. Breathe deeply for a few minutes.

Then discuss what was difficult or easy, how your body responded, what it was like to quiet together.

CLOSE QUIETING

For intimate relationships only: hold someone close. Breathe deeply together for as long as possible. Look into each other's eyes and tell something you appreciate about the other person. See each other through the eyes of Jesus. Add these insights to your appreciation. Bless each other in the name of Jesus.

OBSERVING THROUGH QUIETING

Observe a tense interaction. What were signs of their ability/inability to quiet? What could they have done to restore quiet? What are you learning from this? Share your insights.

QUIETING HELPS

Soft Toy. Some of us find quieting easier if we hold onto something, such as a soft toy. Squeeze it when tense and release it on quieting. It is good to do this in rhythm with quieting prayer.

Cross. A smooth wooden cross helps quieting. Hold on to it and pray: "Thank You, Jesus. You hold on to me."

Foot bath. Massaging your feet in a basin of warm water with the marbles in it helps you to gently focus on His softness, His kindness.

Hand/foot massage. Gentle, slow massage with soothing cream is very healing. No words are necessary, but silent prayer immerses the person in the presence of Jesus.

Colored cloths. Drape people in large cloths of favorite colors and sit together in silence. Different colors have different personal meanings and links to Jesus. Discuss these. One person chose blue for purity and was amazed that Isaiah 61:10 affirmed his purity.

Pictures. Offer a wide selection of pictures for people to choose from to share which one speaks to them something about themselves and Jesus. Ask, "How does this picture help you connect to Jesus?" Turn this into a quieting prayer.

Stations. Around a room place different items to help quieting: e.g., photos, a mirror, a basin of water, a heavy rope, handcuffs, a warm shawl, a candle, or broken tiles. Linger there, then share thoughts of quieting with Jesus.

SCRIPTURES FOR QUIETING PRAYER

Use scriptures for quieting prayer. Personalize these. Say them slowly at least 5 times each so that they become part of your whole being. This is a sure resource for healing and maintaining healing, e.g., "Thank You God, You make everything beautiful in its time" (Ecclesiastes 3:11).

Quieting on the names of God, Jesus, and the Holy Spirit is so helpful for healing. Each name was given for a specific need, to show the unending resources of God's character. You too can connect in specific ways to His unlimited resources. Abba (Father) is one of the hundreds of names to use in quieting prayer. Jesus encountered God as intimate caring Abba in His time of deepest distress before the cross (Mark 14:36). Pray, "God, You are my living, forgiving Abba in my distress" (Galatians 4:6).

BREATHE IN, BREATHE OUT

Sit comfortably and focus on your breathing for a minute. As you breathe in, ask the Holy Spirit to fill you and think of the "breath of God" filling you. Breathe out, asking Jesus to take away any distractions you name. Repeat several times.

Breathe in: "Come, Holy Spirit."

Breathe out: (Name distractions)

Now breathe in, asking Jesus to help you grow different fruits of the Spirit, and breathe out the bad feelings that are the opposite of these fruits. "I breathe in Your love. I breathe in Your joy. I breathe in Your peace. I breathe in Your patience. I breathe in Your kindness. I breathe in Your goodness. I breathe in Your faithfulness. I breathe in Your gentleness. I breathe in Your self-control." Repeat a few times to let Jesus, the Giver of the fruits, fill your whole being.

WEEKLY HEALING CYCLE—GOD'S NAMES

We want to experience the presence of Jesus in everyday life. The Christ-life is to be not just believed or discussed. It is an everyday, all-day experience. The very names Jesus used for Himself encourage us to do this. In the "I am" statements, He fills out the huge mystery of His divinity (John 8:58) with simple street words. He becomes accessible.

Use one "I am" of Jesus for each day. Ponder it. Ask Jesus to show you what aspect of His nature and power He wants you to experience today. Record your experiences.

Day	I AM	Scripture
Sunday	The Bread of Life	John 6:35
Monday	The Light of the World	John 8:12
Tuesday	The Door	John 10:7
Wednesday	The Good Shepherd	John 10:14
Thursday	The Resurrection and the Life	John 11:25
Friday	The Way, the Truth, and the Life	John 14:6
Saturday	The True Vine	John 15:1

WEEKLY HEALING CYCLE—THE FRUITS OF THE SPIRIT
Based on Galatians 5: 22-26

A rhythm of healing develops an antidote to being disconnected or absent—from Jesus, others, and ourselves. This exercise will be an effort, but you will gain greater freedom through choosing to grow the fruits of the Spirit every day. We assign a fruit for each day and associate a color with each fruit. To develop the cycle further, we can ask the Lord to remind us of a story about the fruit for each day and link it to scripture. We can also note the opposite of that fruit. We ask Jesus to grow that fruit more strongly several times during the day as we notice the color that is linked to the fruit.

DAY	FRUIT	SCRIPTURE	COLOR
Sunday	Love	Romans 8:37-39	_____
Monday	Joy	Philippians 2:2	_____
Tuesday	Peace	Isaiah 26:3	_____
Wednesday	Patience	James 1:2-3	_____
Thursday	Faithfulness	Romans 5:1	_____
Friday	Goodness	Ephesians 2:10	_____
Saturday	Self-Control	2 Timothy 1:7	_____

Identify Past Stories of His Presence

Tell your stories in detail, expressing emotions, maintaining eye contact, giving details. Give a name to your stories, a place and a date. Listen attentively to others' stories, clarifying details and helping them connect their stories to the presence of Jesus. These stories build confidence that we know what we are like in the presence of Jesus and how He treated us and will treat us again. We find seeds of healing in our stories.

MY LIFE STORY

Celebrate your story of the presence of Jesus. It is a true story with historical details. In this story, the presence of Jesus reveals your true heart and His character. You affirm together how these healing seeds build confidence in Jesus' ongoing healing. In telling and re-telling this story, you discover more and more of the unique ways Jesus has been and is active in your life for healing.

OUR LIFE STORY

As a group, celebrate a communal story of how members are discovering together new things about themselves and Jesus that they would not have discovered by themselves. As members discover their unity, the value of being together, healing flows in a deeper way. Sharing together leads to gratitude.

APPRECIATION STORIES

Any appreciation story—e. g., of a friend, a place, an animal, a gift, a surprise, some help in crisis, etc.—can help us connect to Jesus. These questions help: What were you like in this story to be appreciated or to show appreciation in this way? How does this connect you to Jesus? Do this with a companion or in a group. Others can then re-tell your appreciation story and say what they see in you and in your connection to Jesus.

BIBLE STORIES

Tell a Bible story, act it out, or draw it—and discuss the theme of the story. Share any of your stories with a similar theme. What links can you make with the Bible story and your story? Your companions will help you. Celebrate how your story fits in with God's wider story.

DRAW YOUR STORY

Draw your story and ask Jesus to accompany you. (e. g., one picture per decade; for each life event; before and after conversion). Color and name each picture. What new aspects of your story emerge? Draw this with a companion and celebrate stories.

TREE OF LIFE STORIES

Share stories of favorite trees, value of trees, or scriptures about trees. Each person draws a large tree making each section clearly with space to write comments. Encourage discussion as you draw.

Roots: Where did you come from? Family history? Names of valued people? Favorite places, songs, games, etc.?

Ground: Where are you now? Current activities? Helpful people? Favorite songs, etc.?

Trunk: your skills and qualities (especially as affirmed by others)

Branches: hopes and dreams

Leaves: significant people alive and dead

Fruits: gifts (from the Holy Spirit) to bless others

Forest of Life: on a large piece of paper, join the drawings of your trees together and see how they fit, their similarities, their effect together as a Forest of Life

Storms of Life: draw in dangers, ways of coping, protections, and note the value of being together, not alone in the Forest of Life

I'D APPRECIATE THIS PERSON IN MY LIFE

Make cards with these names. (They are the names of God in the Psalms from The Message.) Write the reference on the reverse side. Ask members: what kind of person do you need in your life right now?

- Midwife (22:9)
- Singing Teacher (40:2)
- Rock (18:46)
- Rescuing Knight (18:2)
- Safe Leader (31:3)
- Shepherd (23:1)
- High Crag (18:2)
- Cave (31:3)
- High King (95:3)
- Safe Place to Hide (46:1)
- Island Hideaway (32:7)
- Bodyguard (34:20)
- Home (84:1)
- Fountain of cascading light (36:9)

Members choose a name and share the reason for their choice. Then they turn over each card to find that these were names of God in the Psalms. Most are astounded and explained how different is their usual view of God and how different their current dilemmas would be if they hung onto God like this. This leads to short thankful prayers: "Thank You, God. You are my... in my current challenges." "Thank You, God. You are our..."

HEALING SEEDS

Healing seeds in your stories are signs of the presence of Jesus. Tell stories about times when you felt you belonged, acted like yourself, got unstuck from pain, noticed you were growing, or were true to your calling. Celebrate these stories of healing seeds.

COMMUNITY STORIES

List some of the significant events in your community over the last few years. Draw pictures for each event. Is there any common link between these events? Do some themes emerge to help you join the dots (perhaps towards greater connectedness or maturity)? What aspect of Jesus do you celebrate in this theme?

NATURE CONNECTIONS

What what aspects of (or places in) nature help you connect to a healing way to Jesus, others, yourself? How do you foster this? Give examples—through photos, stories, drawings. Pray together: "Remake us in Your beauty" (from a Celtic prayer).

Find Him in Those Moments When He Seemed Absent

When we face blockages to our healing, we reconnect to Jesus with the confidence that we have met Him before in our stories of His presence. None of this is quick, as all growth is slower than we hoped. We make progress, return to former blockages to receive more healing, and then hopefully go on. These tools have helped us to do that with others.

MY TRUE HEART

Discovering the ways God has made you and preserved your true heart under all the stuff of life is healing. Then you understand what your true heart is like and how best to respond to challenges in ways that help you to remain your true self. Use words or images to depict your true heart in Jesus as you discover more and more about it.

TRUE HEARTS OF OTHERS

Honoring the true hearts of others is very healing—for them and us. You begin to look behind their bad behaviors to appreciate how they were created and respond to that. Then you can stay connected to Jesus, others, and ourselves.

GOING ON A BEAR HUNT

The children's story-poem, "We're going on a Bear Hunt,"[47] fits perfectly with how we tend to manage pain. Remember through it as a group if you grew up with it, and bring the book along with you if you can.

The poem goes, "We're going on a bear hunt. / We're gonna catch a big one. / What a beautiful day! / We're not scared." At each obstacle in the book—long wavy grass, a deep cold river, thick oozy mud, a big dark forest, a swirling whirling snowstorm, a narrow gloomy cave—we chant with the story: "We can't go over it. We can't go under it. Oh, no! We've got to go through it!"

Discuss how you face obstacles in life, e. g., avoiding or facing pain. Discuss what helps you go through your pain. Then pray for one another.

POETRY SPEAKS

Poetry can remind us of Jesus' divine presence in the difficult and ordinary. For a starting place, read St. Augustine's "Late Have I Loved You," which describes his arresting encounter with Jesus in the middle of the dissipated lifestyle of his 30s. Then discuss lines that speak to you. Turn those thoughts into healing prayer.

BODY TALK

We forget that Jesus is physically present with us in our bodies! Discuss your exercise regimes (or lack of them), the benefits, the hassles, the challenges. Try some together or reflect with lots of laughter on ones you've done recently (like Chinese dancing).

Admire favorite photos of one another and use Psalm 139:13-18 for appreciation responses. Feel your pulses. Life is running through you. Pause to appreciate life as a gift from God. Examine the unique patterns of our fingertips (using an ink pad—rather messy) to celebrate your created distinctiveness.

Then pause to listen to your bodies. Where is your tension? Do a body scan (Chapter 3). What do you need to know that is already known in your body? Quiet in the presence of Jesus, as it is often hard to encounter body memories. Ask these questions: What is it like to be in your body? What is your body, especially any specific part that is in pain, trying to tell you? What are you trying to ignore? What does your body want to pray right now?

OPPOSITE STORIES

When there are many negative stories, stories of pain, try to remember if there is ever a tiny glimpse (sapphire sparkle) of a story that is/was the opposite of the pain stories (e.g., never loved versus a sign of being loved). Celebrate these stories and ask Jesus what He wants to show about yourselves and His presence in your lives.

RETURN STORY

Tell a story when you were able to return to joy and quiet from one of the Big 6 emotions (anger, fear, disgust, sadness, shame, hopeless despair). Explain what it was like to return to joy. Who helped you? How long did it take? What were the results? Where did you see Jesus in all of this?

LIES OR TRUTH?

Look at these statements. Are they lies or truth? Or a mixture? Suggest truth responses where necessary.

I am the only one who can deal with my pain.

I must avoid/deny pain.

The past can't hurt me if I just move on.

Grief is impossible to heal.

I am beyond self-deception.

I can control my pain.

If you knew my story, you'd see that resentment is justifiable.

Security and predictability are the best choices.

I will never be ready to serve God. I am controlled by my stuff.

Healing should be instant.

I have no power to choose.

I should be capable of forgiving immediately.

NEW YEAR HELPS

Lay out on a table little piles of items for members to choose as encouragers to grow their capacity to face issues in the New Year, even if their circumstances didn't change. They have shopping bags to collect their loot. Items are:

- *Soft balls* – to bounce back as quickly as possible to joy
- *Tissue packs* – to dry tears
- *Fancy buttons* – to press in emergency, to pray, or to ring a friend for help
- *Sandpaper pieces* – to smooth out rough spots (in us first)

- *Promise cards* – to encourage us from God's Word
- *Greeting cards* – to keep in touch with friends
- *Glitter strips* – to remind us to express our creativity
- *Pearls* – to remind us that we are precious and to share the same with others
- *Coffee sachets* – to make sure we have a break
- *Tooth picks* – to pick out our good points and those of others
- *Band-Aids* – for when life hurts
- *Sweets* - to take the bitterness out of life
- *Candles* – to light the way
- *Fun soft toy puppets* – to celebrate the playful child in us
- *Pretty things* – to encourage us to celebrate our beauty
- *Small mirrors* – to see ourselves through the eyes of Jesus, also loved ones, valued group members

As members "shop," stories tumble out about the New Year's fears and hopes. Months later, stories will still tumble out to show these items are helping members to develop resources to face their pain.

MY RETURN TO JOY PLAN

Becoming aware of your tendency to resort to negative emotions is a step towards healing. Returning to joy needs practical steps, and specific help. Write these out. Joy is always relational—with Jesus, others, and yourself.

STORY RESPONSE QUESTIONS

After an unexpected Jesus story (yours or someone else's), explore these questions:

How did Jesus treat you?

What parts of life seemed unconnected to Jesus?

What caused these disconnections?

What effect did these have?

When did you become aware of Jesus as companion and friend in your story?

How did quieting help this process?

What were you like in the presence of Jesus?

What thoughts and changes occurred when you linked your pain story with your presence of Jesus story?

Express Thanks to Him

Expressing thanks to Jesus for the amazing way He has placed healing seeds in your stories is your natural response to being immersed in His presence. You want to live in His presence, to keep growing and asking Him into your ongoing pain.

MY/OUR CONTINUING LIFE STORY

Record and celebrate ongoing stories of practicing the presence of Jesus, the subsequent life changes, and those who affirm these changes. Do this as a group as well.

MEMENTOS OF GOD'S KINDNESS

Track objects, people, and places that remind you of God's presence, His kindness. These are like the Old Testament memorials that keep you connected to God in a very practical way.

LIVING OUT OF MY LIFE STORY

In writing or pictures, link the discoveries in your LIFE story to any current challenges. Creating a certificate helps link the discoveries in your LIFE Story to current challenges. It encourages you to encounter Jesus in His healing ways again, so the healing journey can continue.

I USED TO...BUT NOW...

Growth is worth celebrating and exploring. We like to do this in groups or in writing by filling in the phrase, "I used to... but now..." Bob Goff lists over 200 of these in his book, *Love Does*,[48] which we use to stimulate our own:

- I used to think Jesus motivated us by ultimatums, but now I know He pursues us in love.

- I used to think that clenched fists helped me fight better, but now I know they make me weaker.

- I used to think mission needed a program to define it, but now I just respond to the Father who says, "Come."

Then we share ours and celebrate our growing in maturity.

CONNECTING PRAYER

Pray this prayer daily to keep connecting to Jesus. It's modeled on the "Gospel Prayer" by J. D. Greear[49]:

> Lord Jesus, there is nothing I can do that would make You love me more. There is nothing I have done that makes You love me less.
>
> Your presence is all I need to build joy-filled relationships.
>
> All You have been to me, so I will be to others.
>
> As I pray, I'll measure Your compassion by the cross and Your power by Your resurrection.

WITH WHOM?

Our aim is to live in the presence of Jesus. Read this phrase: "In my life, what matters is not where, not what... but with Whom." How are you discovering this?

LIFE MELODY

What song represents your life melody? What song helps you deal with the unresolvable in life?

THE PAIN PROCESSING PATHWAY

What insights for prayer healing do you gain from the process in Appendix C? Why are words of advice only helpful at level 5 of the pain processing pathway? How does awareness of maturity blockages help the healing process?

MYSTERIES

What are the mysteries and unfinished parts of your story?

What helps you accept these?

What happens when your story theme and the biblical theme don't seem to connect? What helps you connect?

HIS HAND

Skip Moen gives another version of Psalm 73:23: "You grasped my right hand. I couldn't do it. I was falling over the edge. You had to grab me."[50] What stories do you have of God or His people grabbing you to direct you into His ways of living, responding?

TRUE HEART

Discovering the true heart of the abuser behind its malfunction helps the forgiving process.

Tell a story:

> When did someone hurt you? How bad was this?

What did you think of that person? How did it affect your relationship?

What was malfunctioning in their heart? What would they do if they were acting from the heart Jesus gave them?

What happens to you when you focus on their true heart? How does this help you recover from any of the BIG 6 emotions (anger, fear, shame, disgust, sadness, or hopeless despair)?

How does this help you act in a way consistent with the heart Jesus gave you? Ask Jesus for His help.

What does it mean for you to "forgive from your heart"?

[47] Michael Rosen and Helen Oxenbury, *We're Going on a Bear Hunt* (London: Walker Books, 1989).
[48] Bob Goff, *Love Does: Discover a Secretly Incredible Life in an Ordinary World* (Nashville: Thomas Nelson, 2012).
[49] J. D. Greear, "The Gospel Prayer," *JDGreear.com*, August 27, 2016, accessed November 14, 2016, *www.jdgreear.com/my_weblog/2016/08/the-gospel-prayer.html*.
[50] Skip Moen, "Get a Grip," *Hebrew Word Study*, May 2, 2012, accessed November 14, 2016, *skipmoen.com/2012/05/get-a-grip/*.

APPENDIX C: THE PAIN PROCESSING PATHWAY

Neuroscientists Karl Lehman and Jim Wilder have helped us to understand the God-created plasticity of our brain and its discernible pathway to pain processing.[51] In Chapter 6, "Seeds of Healing," we identified the questions that mark this pathway as we have come to understand and use them. Here is a more thorough (though still quite simplified) discussion of those six questions—the signs that they are unresolved, and the places we might look to find healing seeds of answers to them.

Do I Belong?

- *Need:* Joy, connection, support

- *Deficit Cries:* I feel as though no one is supporting me. No one looks at me with joy, and I have no one with whom to build joy. My friendships (if any) don't seem to be very meaningful. I either cling to people or dismiss them entirely.

- *Skill Needed:* Secure attachments

- *Helps for Finding & Growing Seeds:* Joy-building stories and exercises

- *Seeds Found in Stories of:* the explicit presence of Jesus; unexpected support; secure, joyful relationships; unconditional love.

Am I Safe?

- *Need:* Quiet to discover internal resources to meet challenges

- *Deficit Cries:* I live in fear, not love. I just want it to stop. I look for coping mechanisms outside of myself (possibly through self-medication and addiction) because I can't calm myself down when faced with trauma and challenges.

- *Skills Needed:* Self-calming

- *Helps for Finding & Growing Seeds:* Quieting prayer and exercises, extended quieting

- *Seeds Found in Stories of:* moments when internal resources were enough, when addictions were avoided, when I acted like myself

Am I Stuck?

- *Need:* Connection with healthy others

- *Deficit Cries:* When I face the "big six" emotions (anger, fear, shame, disgust, sadness, hopeless despair), I isolate myself. I don't deserve to relate to others in this state, but I want someone to understand me. I don't know how to get out.

- *Skill Needed:* Staying relational even in pain

- *Helps for Finding & Growing Seeds:* Regular companionship, community (joy groups), ways to return to joy
- *Seeds Found in Stories of:* relating even in times of trauma, moments when I asked for help or connected with others in joy instead of isolating

Am I Growing?

- *Need:* Sense of personal growth, self-efficacy; models to grow toward
- *Deficit Cries:* I'm not confident that I'm handling things well even at my best. I feel as though some foundational gaps are holding back my development. I wish I could do better. I'm not sure where or how to grow from here.
- *Skills Needed:* Acting like oneself
- *Helps for Finding & Growing Seeds:* Look to role models, those who inspire and support
- *Seeds Found in Stories of:* growth, epiphanies, how I have changed, been supported, contributed to the growth of others

Am I Living From My True Heart?

- *Need:* Strong sense of identity and calling
- *Deficit Cries:* I'm unsure of who I'm supposed to be; I live more in lies than in His truth. I can't get a sense of the themes or purpose of my life. I need to produce lasting fruit for His Kingdom.

- *Skills Needed:* Receiving, living in truth

- *Helps for Finding & Growing Seeds:* God's truth, hearing how Jesus sees me, applying helpful advice from others (Note: this is the ONLY stage where advice helps!)

- *Seeds Found in Stories of:* glimpses of my true heart and calling; times when my unique identity was part of the solution, as it helped me and others suffer well, and live from the basis of God's truth

---

[51] For more information on the work of Karl Lehman and Jim Wilder, see their websites: *www.kclehman.com* and *www.lifemodel.org.*

BIBLIOGRAPHY

Bonhoeffer, Dietrich. *I Want to Live These Days with You: A Year of Daily Devotions*. Louisville: Westminster John Knox Press, 2007.

Calvin, John. *Institutes, Book 1*. Translated by Henry Beveridge. Edinburgh: Calvin Translation Society, 1845.

Dix, Gregory. *The Shape of the Liturgy*. London: Dacre Press, 1945.

Doidge, Norman. *The Brain That Changes Itself*. London: Penguin, 2007.

Eldridge, John. *Desire*. Nashville: Thomas Nelson, 2007.

Frost, Michael. *Exiles: Living Missionally in a Post-Christian Culture*. Erina, NSW: Strand, 2006.

Goff, Bob. *Love Does: Discover a Secretly Incredible Life in an Ordinary World*. Nashville: Thomas Nelson, 2012.

Greear, J. D. "The Gospel Prayer." *JDGreear.com*, August 27, 2016. Accessed November 14, 2016. *www.jdgreear.com/my_weblog/2016/08/the-gospel-prayer.html*.

Lawrence, Brother, and Frank Laubach. *Practicing His Presence*. Edited by G. Edwards. Jacksonville: Seedsowers, 1973.

L'Engle, Madeleine. *Walking on Water: Reflections on Faith and Art*. Colorado Springs: Waterbrook Press, 2001.

Lehman, Karl. "Identifying When You Have Lost Access to Your Relational Connection Circuits, and Getting Them Back On Line," November 12, 2008. Accessed November 12, 2016. *www.kclehman.com/download.php?doc=151*.

Lehman, Karl. *Outsmarting Yourself: Catching Your Past Invading the Present and What to Do About It*. Libertyville: This JOY! Books, 2011.

Manning, Brennan. *Abba's Child: The Cry of the Heart for Intimate Belonging*. Colorado Springs: NavPress, 1994.

Moen, Skip. *Hebrew Word Study*. Accessed November 14, 2016. *www.skipmoen.com*.

Rosen, Michael, and Helen Oxenbury, *We're Going on a Bear Hunt*. London: Walker Books, 1989.

Schacter, Daniel. "Remembering the Past to Imagine the Future: The Prospective Brain." *Nature Reviews Neuroscience 8* (2007): 657-661.

Thompson, Curt. *Anatomy of the Soul: Surprising Connections between Neuroscience and Spiritual Practices That Can Transform Your Life and Relationships*. Wheaton: Tyndale, 2010.

Underhill, Evelyn. *Light of Christ: Addresses Given at the House of Retreat Pleshey, in May 1932*. Eugene: Wipf and Stock, 2004.

White, Andrew. *Faith under Fire*. Grand Rapids: Monarch Books, 2011.

Wilder, Jim, et al. *Living from the Heart Jesus Gave You*. Pasadena: Shepherd's House, 2004.

Wright, N. T. *The Challenge of Jesus*. London: SPCK, 2000.

SERVANT PARTNERS PRESS
Proclaiming God's Presence among the Urban Poor

Servant Partners Press is dedicated to supporting the growing movement of people who are called to live and work alongside the urban poor. We publish theological reflections, narratives, and training materials that speak to God's transforming power in the inner cities and slums of our world.

To learn more about Servant Partners Press or to purchase books, visit us at *ServantPartnersPress.org*.

www.ingramcontent.com/pod-product-compliance
Lightning Source LLC
Chambersburg PA
CBHW032136020426
42334CB00016B/1181